Redescribing Reality

Other books by Walter Brueggemann

Praying the Psalms, 2nd edition

Ichabod toward Home: The Journey of God's Glory

In Man We Trust: The Neglected Side of Biblical Faith

To Act Justly, Love Tenderly, Walk Humbly: An Agenda for Ministers

Theology of the Old Testament: Testimony, Dispute, Advocacy

Old Testament Theology: Essays on Structure, Theme, and Text

Like Fire in the Bones: Listening for the Prophetic Word in Jeremiah

The Word that Describes the World: The Bible and Discipleship

The Word Militant: Preaching a Decentering World

Awed to Heaven, Rooted to Earth: Prayers of Walter Brueggemann

The Book That Breathes New Life: Scriptural Authority and Biblical Theology

Interpretation and Obedience: From Faithful Reading to Faithful Living

Redescribing Reality

What We do when We Read the Bible

Walter Brueggemann

scm press

© Walter Brueggemann 2009

First published in the US in 2008, entitled *A Pathway of Interpretation*,
by Cascade Books

Published in the UK in 2009 by SCM Press
Editorial office
13–17 Long Lane,
London, EC1A 9PN, UK

First published in the US in 2008 as *A Pathway of Interpretation:
The Old Testament for Pastors and Students* by Cascade Books, a Division of
Wipf&Stock Publishers, 199 W.8th Ave., Suite 3, Eugene, OR, 97401, USA.

SCM Press is an imprint of Hymns Ancient and Modern Ltd (a registered charity)
St Mary's Works, St Mary's Plain,
Norwich, NR3 3BH, UK
www.scm-canterburypress.co.uk

British Library Cataloguing in Publication data

A catalogue record for this book is available
from the British Library

978 0 334 04216 7

Printed in the UK by
CPI William Clowes Beccles NR34 7TL

To Frederick R. Trost

CONTENTS

ACKNOWLEDGMENTS

I AM GLAD TO DEDICATE THIS BOOK TO FRED TROST, MY LONG-TIME companion in church theology. Fred does the kind of biblical-pastoral reflection that I think matters the most and is the most responsible. Well beyond his critical competence, his work is marked by large-hearted generosity and passion concerning the tough justice questions. Fred has been my conversation partner for many decades, and I grateful for his unfailing courage alongside his deep graciousness. I have no doubt that Fred embodies the best gifts of the evangelical tradition of the Kirchenverein from which we both have sprung, and I greet him in gratitude and affection.

I have completed this manuscript with two large waves of gratitude. First, K.C. Hanson not only suggested this writing project to me and has seen it through to publication. In addition he has done major work on the pages, and has done the hard, careful work on the bibliography. Second, Tia Foley has attended to the complex matters of retrieving the old journal articles and piecing together my new work in relation to them to bring the book to fruition. Without her persistence and diligence, the book would not have been completed. On both counts, I am deeply grateful.

PREFACE

I WAS PLEASED WHEN K. C. HANSON SUGGESTED THAT I WRITE A BOOK on my own work with particular attention to methodological issues. I have found this writing not at all easy for at least two reasons. First, nobody likes to go back to see what they have previously written, for very often one can quickly see how it should have been done better than it was. But the second reason for the difficulty is that my work is largely intuitive and homiletical or, in the words of Carolyn Sharp, marked by "characteristic ebullient romanticization." I have not often lingered over methodological issues, but have moved ahead with a sense of urgency concerning the "main chance" of the text.

To go back now to reflect on method is a sobering experience. I have done so because I have wanted to explore with some care a responsible way of textual interpretation that takes seriously both critical learning and confessional passion but that is not so preoccupied as to be drawn away from the text itself by methodological issues. When sound method is disregarded, we often get a reductive rationalism or a reductive creedalism. Either reductionism clearly fails to attend to the cunning detail and summoning nerve that characteristically occur in the text.

This attempt to reflect on method has permitted me to review my own personal history and the ways in which I have been nurtured in a particular style of interpretation. I am aware that my approach to interpretive method has not been satisfying or acceptable in some quarters among my colleagues. My work has been notably critiqued by two recently deceased scholars: from the "canonical" perspective of Brevard S. Childs, and from the "scientific" perspective of James Barr, who has regarded interpretation with reference to faith as a betrayal of our proper critical work.[1] I have

---

1. The strictures concerning my work include the following: Childs, "Walter Brueggemann's *Theology of the Old Testament. Testimony, Dispute, Advocacy*"; and Barr,

learned a great deal from Professors Childs and Barr and the perspectives they represent; but I have not been able to sign on with either perspective in a complete way. I have kept on with my intuitive way of reading because my engagement with church pastors and church lay folk (and seminarians) indicates to me that my way of working has been generative, empowering, and summoning, even if it does not always meet the more rigorous requirements of some colleagues in the guild.

In these introductory comments I want to report on what I have been learning about my own personal history with reference to the text and its interpretation. I would encourage you to reflect on how your own heritage, upbringing, religious and academic training, and mentors have influenced your reading of Scripture.

The Social Gospel

I grew up in an all-containing church culture of the old Evangelical and Reformed Church, a church culture that was passionate and self-aware, but without any hint of theological authoritarianism. My father was a pastor in that church, who baptized me, nurtured and confirmed me in faith, and eventually ordained me.

My father, no great intellect, was a faithful interpreter of the Bible. He had been educated at Eden Theological Seminary, a school of the old Evangelical Synod that had committed to the historical-critical study of the Bible from its earliest years. For the most part there were no battles in my church about historical criticism and literalism, and no theological "tests" were imposed or contested. The learning of "guild scholarship" was taken as a useful tool in a "soft" read of Scripture. The other dimension of my father's education is that he was a child of the Social Gospel, in the same church tradition out of which Reinhold Niebuhr had emerged. My father had, through his ministerial life, a passion for social justice. In the years just after my father's ordination in 1925, the Evangelical Catechism was revised. The first question remained the same in the new edition, "What is man's chief concern?" The old answer was, "Man's chief concern is the eternal salvation of his soul," reflecting a strong pietistic perspective. But the new answer in 1929, under the impetus of the Social Gospel became, "Man's chief concern is to seek after the Kingdom of God and

_____

The Concept of Biblical Theology, 540–62.

his righteousness." The new answer very much reflected the theological, interpretive perspective of my father that was committed to neighborly questions of justice. Along with historical criticism and a passion for justice, it is to be noted that the term that most characterized that church tradition was "irenic," again reflective of a background of pietism. There were few interpretive quarrels in the church, few blatant impositions of ideology, though there were the unexamined interpretive assumptions of an immigrant community.

Between Orthodoxy and Rationalism

I have referred to the pietistic background of my tradition, a consideration of which pushes me back behind my immediate familial and church nurture to identify the interpretive perspective in which I am situated. My childhood church, the Evangelical and Reformed Church and its Midwestern antecedent, the Evangelical Synod North America, was a church that was brought with the immigrant community from Germany. The German church from which the immigrants came was the Evangelical Church of the Prussian Union, a church formed in 1817 when the King of Prussia required Lutherans and Calvinists in his realm to cease their theological quarrels in order to live together in the same church.[2] Of necessity that newly formed church eschewed any narrowly confessional claim, Lutheran or Calvinist, and lived from a shared piety that permitted choice in the face of confessional differences. That church, for which Frederick Schleiermacher was the formative theologian, was grounded in pietism that was committed to an innocent, simple trust in the Jesus of the Gospels without needing to settle all the theological issues implied in an affirmation of Jesus. That pietism, marked by an irenic spirit, eschewed the kind of hardnosed confessionalism of the "orthodox" Lutherans and Calvinists who, within a century, had hardened the claims of the Reformation in formulaic ways. Calvinistic scholasticism was something of a force in Germany; but a more toxic confessionalism was practiced by the Lutherans, a confessionalism that came to the United States in the form of Missouri Synod Lutheranism. It is the case that the Evangelical Synod

2. The founding of the Prussian Union in 1817 was an act quite consciously taken on the 300th anniversary of Luther's famous Wittenberg challenge to the church that is commonly taken as the initiation of "the Reformation."

functioned concretely as a "soft" Reformation church that was regularly juxtaposed to the Missouri Synod, often "the other church" in town.[3]

This church, committed to pietism, also resisted *rationalism* that was evoked as a reaction to *orthodox scholasticism*. Rationalism sought to recast faith in ways amenable to Enlightenment rationality, an enterprise that continues in current attempts to distinguish Jesus from the "mythological" and "miraculous" in which the gospel narratives cast him. When the immigrants came to the United States, there were "free thinking" German rationalists who looked askance at the church (my grandfather was among them). Positioned as the church was vis-à-vis orthodoxy and rationalism, the option of pietism appealed more to a passionate "experience" of trust in Jesus than the hard-edged thinking of the alternatives of orthodoxy and rationalism. It was this pietism that created the ethos of the church and evoked and sustained a benign community of faith and witness.

An "Innocent" Perspective

Only lately have I reread a study of the transplanting of the church from Prussia to the Midwest of the United States. In his superb Yale dissertation of 1952, David George Gelzer explored the way in which German pastors were dispatched by the Basel Mission House to serve the German immigrant communities in the United States.[4] The Mission House was founded in the early nineteenth century precisely to nurture missionary pastors. The ethos of the Mission House was committed to church union that resisted every attempt at confessionalism. It was pastors from the Mission House who in 1840 convened the *Kirchenverein* in suburban St. Louis that was to grow to become the Evangelical Synod and then the Evangelical and Reformed Church.[5] It is of great importance that this

3. This particular trajectory of the Reformation was primally informed by Philip Melanchthon, Luther's close associate, who was a temporizing, reconciling figure in the development of Reformation teaching.

4. Gelzer, "Mission to America being A History of the Work of the Basel Foreign Mission Society in America." While Gelzer's subject is the Basel Mission House, he makes clear that the Barmen Mission House was also important for what became the *Kirchenverein*.

5. The Evangelical and Reformed Church in 1957 became a part of the United Church of Christ.

founding community in the United States was not a "church," but was a *Verein*, a fellowship of pastors whose accent was on the missional task and not on theological formulation or organizational structure. Indeed it was assumed—and continued to be assumed in the Evangelical Synod—that a unionist Reformation consensus of the gospel was accepted and did not need to be reformulated and certainly did not need to be disputed.

I take notice of the antecedents of the Prussian Union, the *Kirchenverein*, and the Evangelical Synod because I am increasingly aware that my father was a faithful practitioner of the unionist interpretive tradition that was uninterested in particularized theological formulation and that understood theological thought as a tool for faithful missional ministry. The gospel to which this tradition was committed concerned Jesus as healer and redeemer. There was not much troubling about critical questions or theological niceties.[6] As I ponder this interpretive tradition, the term that occurs to me is "innocence," a stance that I have continued in my own interpretation. The temptations of "orthodoxy" and "rationalism" continue to reappear in current interpretation and in Old Testament study, perhaps with reference to various forms of "canonical" and "critical" study, and I have, unwittingly, continued to practice the "innocent" perspective of my tradition. One result of that "innocence" is that I am often taken by surprise by critical questions that had not occurred to me or by issues that I had carelessly disregarded because I was not alert to the complexity. I believe that I have been rather consistently focused on what I have taken to be the "main point" and have been unconcerned about all sorts of matters that the more "orthodox" and more "rationalistic" interpreters have been able to identify.

My Path in Old Testament Studies

In my education in college, seminary, and graduate school, I stayed closer to this interpretive tradition than I understood at the time. At Elmhurst College I took on only the required courses in Bible and focused on sociology, history, and philosophy. When I began work at Eden Seminary (where my father had graduated in 1925, and where I graduated with

---

6. Evidence for resistance to any confessional stance is found in the fact that Eden Seminary, until after World War II, had no faculty chair in Systematic Theology. That chair was first created when Allen O. Miller came to the faculty.

my brother Ed in 1958), I was drawn to Old Testament studies by the uncommon teachers available to me. My first teacher of Old Testament was Allen G. Wehrli, who had been my father's teacher as well.[7] He was an uncommonly learned man who had studied under Hermann Gunkel at Halle and with William Foxwell Albright at John Hopkins University; but he wore his learning lightly.[8] The pedagogical experience with Wehrli was through mesmerizing storytelling in which, with modest but uncompromising attention to critical matters, he inducted us into the wonder and mystery and hiddenness of the biblical narrative.[9] He fulfilled the first obligation of a good teacher, namely, to leave students interested in the subject wanting more.

My second seminary teacher in Old Testament, who eventually influenced me more, was Lionel Whiston Jr. He came to the seminary faculty with a Harvard degree. Fully schooled in critical matters, it turned out that he was primarily interested in the artistic and dramatic dimensions of the biblical text, and was concerned to find analogues, parallels, and reiterations of biblical themes in contemporary culture. It was Whiston who introduced us to the work of Gerhard von Rad, that great German interpreter who redefined the interpretive task in his poetic idiom and theological passion that arose in the context of the German Confessing Church in the 1930s. The excitement of the interpretive project from von Rad via Whiston was my impetus for further study.[10] It is clear that both Wehrli and Whiston, schooled in historical criticism, had other vistas of interpretation that concerned, respectively, the imaginative faithfulness of the church and the healthiness of human culture.

7. I am glad to add that Eugene S. Wehrli, son of Allen Wehrli my teacher, friend, colleague, and eventually president of Eden Seminary, fully embodied the ethos of the *Kirchenverein* tradition. He combined an irenic spirit, a critical erudition, and a simple pietism in thought and life.

8. I do wonder how many other Old Testament scholars studied with both Gunkel and Albright. I suspect their number is very few, but there is no way to know. I imagine that Wehrli was distinctive in this regard.

9. After studying with Wehrli, I discovered, when I began graduate work, that in his storytelling in Introduction, Wehrli had in fact given us a complete taxonomy of Gunkel's *Gattungen* (genres), a classification that Wehrli had disguised in his artful narrative skill.

10. Along with these teachers, a decisive influence for my entry into Old Testament study was the little book by B. Napier, *From Faith to Faith*. Napier's book was among the first renderings in English of the new work by Gerhard von Rad that electrified my awareness of the Old Testament as a theological enterprise.

I matriculated in Union Theological Seminary in New York for doctoral work largely at the behest of Whiston. Completely by happenstance and previously unknown to me, my major teacher and eventually my *Doktorvater* was James Muilenburg, who, in his generation of Old Testament scholars, was "not like the others."[11] In those years at Union Seminary, Muilenburg was exploring what became his proposal for "rhetorical criticism" with primary attention to the detail of the text without excessive reference to more conventional historical criticism.[12] Muilenburg himself grasped and enacted the dramatic power of the text and left us regularly dazzled as he opened the text for us with its rhetorical

---

11. Frederick Buechner has written passionately about the impact of James Muilenburg on him and on many of us:

"Every morning when you wake up," he used to say, "before you reaffirm your faith in the majesty of a loving God, before you say *I believe* for another day, read the *Daily News* with its record of the latest crimes and tragedies of mankind and then see if you can honestly say it again." He was a fool in the sense that he didn't or couldn't or wouldn't resolve, intellectualize, evade, the tensions of his faith but lived those tensions out, torn almost in two by them at times. He was a fool, I suppose, in the sense that he was an intimate of the dark, yet held fast to the light as if it were something you could hold fast to; in the sense that he wore his heart on his sleeve even though it was in some ways a broken heart; in the sense that he was as absurdly himself before the packed lecture hall as he was alone in his office; a fool in the sense that he was a child in his terrible candor. A fool, in other words, for Christ. (*Now and Then*, 16–17)

Of this characterization Dale Brown, *The Book of Buechner*, 81, comments:

This extended picture of Muilenburg is important, not only because of his enormous influence on *The Return of Ansel Gibbs*, but also because Muilenburg was, demonstrably, the model Buechner chooses for himself. Gibbs will choose Kuykendall just as Buechner has chosen Muilenburg. Tillich and Niebuhr and others are undoubtedly central as later influences such as Kierkegaard and C. S. Lewis and Graham Greene will be, but Muilenburg contributes something of the soul to Buechner. Buechner's current popularity as a lecturer derives in part, I submit, from his internalization of Muilenburg's style and ideology. Notice in the description of Muilenburg's peculiar power the emphasis on personal honesty, willingness to be self-revealing, dedication to intense faith despite the presence of overwhelming darkness—trademarks of Buechner's own writing and preaching. Muilenburg's influence was that of a prophet, an intense, maybe even deranged, bringer of the Word. It was certainly Muilenburg whom Buechner has in mind when he alleges, "In the last analysis, I have always believed, it is not so much their subjects that the great teachers teach as it is themselves."

12. See Muilenburg, "Form Criticism and Beyond." For a careful and insightful commentary on Muilenburg's program, see Trible, *Rhetorical Criticism*.

power that did not allow its poetic force to be curbed either by confessional certitude or by rational flatness.

As I reflect now on the impact on me of Wehrli, Whiston, and Muilenburg—each in an idiosyncratic way—I have the growing conviction that I was schooled in formal modes of interpretation that are quite congruent with the "innocence" of my own particular tradition of interpretation from Basel and the *Verein*. There was, to be sure, a full induction into the specificities of historical criticism. I understood then and understand now the cruciality of historical criticism that serves to prevent the scripture from being hijacked for any particular ideology.[13] While historical criticism is not in any full sense "objective," it does function as a check on extensive forms of subjectivism. Given that, however, such criticism is not and cannot be the end or goal of serious interpretation of the Bible when it is taken as scripture.[14] Thus my interest in method is to take historical criticism seriously, but not to linger over it. When historical criticism is practiced properly, it may be a tool for moving along toward serious theological interpretation that is responsible, even if committed.[15]

Teaching and Fresh Hermeneutical Challenges

When I began my teaching vocation at Eden Theological Seminary in 1961, I was, as were all of the fresh generation of Old Testament teachers to which I belong, generally unbothered about the interface of historical criticism and "belief-full" interpretation. Most of us in my generation were scholars nurtured in church contexts and who were to return to those contexts as teachers. Along with my many Old Testament colleagues of that generation, I have continued to live at the interface of criticism

13. I became aware of how crucial historical criticism is during the 1970s at my time at Eden Seminary. During those days, our colleague seminary, Concordia Seminary, was in the hotbox wherein the reactionary forces of Missouri Synod Lutheranism threatened and took over the seminary. In that splendid faculty that was displaced, historical criticism was an important resource by which to fend off ideology posing as interpretation. At Eden Seminary, by contrast, there was no need for such a defense, and for that reason historical criticism in that context was not nearly so urgent.

14. Levenson, *The Hebrew Bible, the Old Testament, and Historical Criticism*, has probed the problematic interface of faith and criticism in a shrewd and discerning way.

15. Many scholars now agree that the matter is not an either/or but a both/and. Excessive polemic has been voiced from both sides; but in the end the work to be done includes both criticism and "beyond criticism."

and faith. In my first decade of teaching, moreover, the urgency of faithful interpretation for the church was given impetus by Vatican II that was an enormous occasion for us all, not least opening conversations with new colleagues from the Roman Catholic Church.

Before a decade was past, the easy interface of criticism and faith was interrupted and called into question in an abrasive way. The social environment of the U.S. church (and its seminaries) received a rude wake-up call through a series of "disruptions" that revolved around 1968: the Paris student revolts, the Democratic National Convention in Chicago, the assassinations of Bobby Kennedy and Martin Luther King Jr., and the broader issues of Civil Rights, Vietnam, and Watergate. This series of disruptions called into question the taken-for-granted paradigms of interpretation. Those paradigms had assumed that there was no unmanageable tension between criticism and faith. This assumption was now seriously called into question.

In that matrix of dislocation, fresh hermeneutical challenges emerged that may be roughly grouped around the theme of liberation, challenges that featured Latin American liberation, feminism, and eventually, post-colonial interpretation. My own first serious engagement was through the work of José Miranda in 1974.[16] That broad challenge to conventional interpretive assumptions exposed critical scholarship as an advocate alongside other advocacies, and not, as was widely assumed, an objective read of the texts. Such criticism functions, willy-nilly, to challenge conventional church authoritarianism as an advocacy for Enlightenment rationality whereby the Bible could accommodate dominant reason. Indeed given such a critical stance, whenever readers found a tension or contradiction in the text of the Old Testament, the "problem" was characteristically resolved by positing distinct "sources," a move that inevitably cut the nerve of artistic tension that was often the very intent of the text. (One can see this same operation still at work in New Testament scholarship whereby texts that are "problematic" are taken from Jesus and assigned to the early church.)

In the 1970s I engaged in a long season of team teaching at Eden Seminary with M. Douglas Meeks. Meeks introduced me to the Critical Theory of the Frankfurt School and instructed me in the capacity of theological interpretation to raise critical questions about social reality that

16. Miranda, *Marx and the Bible*.

were characteristically muted in conventional historical criticism. At the same time, by happenstance, I began to read Paul Ricoeur. I began with *Freud and Philosophy*, where Ricoeur identifies a "hermeneutic of suspicion" and a "hermeneutic of retrieval."[17] Eventually Ricoeur permitted me to think again about imagination, though I had already written *Prophetic Imagination* before I happened onto Ricoeur.[18] Since then I have, for a very long time, worked on understanding imagination as a practice of interpretation that required me to move out beyond the methods in which I had been inducted.[19] I have come to see that *imagination* is the capacity to entertain, host, trust, and respond to *images* of reality (God and the world) that are out beyond conventional dominant reason. Its has slowly dawned on me that biblical exposition cannot be, in the context of the church, a scientific enterprise designed to recover the past as historical criticism has attempted; it is an artistic preoccupation that is designed to generate alternative futures.[20]

Eventually it became clear to me that Ricoeur's "second naiveté" is exactly the point of the work that I am able to do.[21] By that phrase Ricoeur refers to readiness to take the Bible seriously as Scripture—as authoritative revelation—after one has abandoned a first simplistic naiveté and after one has seriously engaged criticism and pushed it as far as one can go. "Second naiveté" comes along with a full awareness of the epistemological crisis caused for faith by Enlightenment rationality. It does not invite a refusal to think critically, nor does it offer an option of being dishonest about the facts on the ground. It recognizes that in the midst of such rationality, there is nonetheless a "surplus" that cannot be vetoed by critical thought, but that continues to be generative when the text is heard in a kind of truthful innocence.[22] As I reflected on the *practice of imagination* and *the*

17. Paul Ricoeur, *Freud and Philosophy*.

18. Brueggemann, *The Prophetic Imagination* (1st ed. 1978; 2nd ed. 2001).

19. Of my several discussions of imagination, see especially *Hopeful Imagination* and *Texts under Negotiation*.

20. Paul Ricoeur has phrased this work as a concern for "the world in front of the text," on which see Stiver, *Theology after Ricoeur*, 63–66. For an intense argument that we move beyond historical criticism (or back behind historical criticism) to a more generative approach, see Jason Byassee, *Praise Seeking Understanding*. See also the recent discussion of Kugel, *How to Read the Bible*.

21. For a summary and review of Ricoeur's notion of "second naiveté," see Wallace, *The Second Naiveté*.

22. As far as I am aware, Ricoeur first utilized the notion of "surplus" in *Interpretation*

capacity for second naiveté, it occurred to me that Ricoeur has supplied phrasing for what has been operative in my nurture from my father and Wehrli and Whiston and Muilenburg and, indirectly, from von Rad.

In terms of my continuing education, I should note that 1978–1979 were momentous years in Old Testament study. In 1978 my teacher, Samuel Terrien, published his elegant proposal for "a new Biblical theology" in which he juxtaposed the ethical and the aesthetic.[23] His book has not received much attention, but it is important as an act of courage that asserted that such Old Testament theology was possible after the intellectual disability of the 1970s. In 1979, two books appeared that changed the field of Old Testament study and that impacted me heavily. On the one hand, Brevard S. Childs published his introduction to the Old Testament "as Scripture," by which he meant that the Bible is to be studied with reference to its intentional theological claim.[24] After that book, Childs went on to his "canonical" study, but that book seems to me to be the decisive turn in his work.[25] On the other hand, Norman K. Gottwald published *The Tribes of Yahweh* in which he analyzed the sociological intentionality of the early traditions of Israel with reference to its ideological angle.[26] While Gottwald himself sought to articulate an interface between his book and that of Childs, it is the case that the two books sketched out the decisive trajectories of interpretation that would occupy the field for the following decades.[27] I have found it possible and necessary to take both enterprises seriously, because I believe that the passionate claims that Gottwald has seen as *ideology* are in fact the intention of the *canonical* in Childs's horizon. The recognition that the canon is an intense partisan claim permits us to see the radicality of the text to which the church is always playing catch-up. It is impossible to overstate the importance of these two books

---

Theory; on his later development of the theme, see Stiver, *Theology after Ricoeur*, chapter 3. Recently Rieger, *Christ and Empire*, has taken up the theme of "surplus" as the continuing claim of the Gospel in the text after the text is seen to be fully permeated by imperial ideology. Rieger's argument is that even the power of ideology cannot defeat the claims of the Gospel. His usage is somewhat different from that of Ricoeur, but the two uses will be gainfully considered together.

23. Terrien, *The Elusive Presence*.

24. Childs, *Introduction to the Old Testament as Scripture*.

25. Childs's "canonical" program culminated in *Biblical Theology of the Old and New Testaments*.

26. Gottwald, *The Tribes of Yahweh*.

27. Gottwald, "Social Matrix and Canonical Shape."

for my education and for my continuing effort to move beyond historical questions.

I have spoken of the "innocence" of the pietistic tradition of the *Kirchenverein* that did not seek out quarrels about or precision concerning theological formulation. That tradition trusted the simplest, most elemental claims of the Gospel that it understood quite experientially.[28] That innocence, in my theological tradition, was able to take seriously and absorb historical criticism without abandoning its rough theological consensus. And I have spoken of Ricoeur's "second naiveté," a capacity for trustful affirmation even in a knowing world of rational thought and uncommon violence. I do not equate that ancient *innocence* with contemporary *naiveté*, but I believe that in my particular interpretive tradition they are in remarkable ways in continuity with one another.

The outcome of this tradition of innocence-become-naiveté is a readiness to hear the biblical text and to be led, as much as our defining social limits permit, to its compelling alternative voice in the world. That outcome, which I seek to detail in the essays that follow in this collection, has required of me that I take seriously the fruits of criticism without taking them as the final act of interpretation. In parallel fashion, it has required of me that I be much informed by a canonical approach, without following it to the logical outcome of an imposition of a doctrinal form on the biblical text, because I do not believe such a move takes the text itself with sufficient seriousness. I conclude that my interpretive tradition—in a way congruent with my own personal inclination—is to live between canonical and critical, and to listen in faith that goes beyond the reach of criticism or the certitude of canon. I believe that this is how the church must live in response to the text; the church, in its deepest moments of

---

28. The simplicity of the theological tradition of the *Kirchenverein* is nicely exhibited in the final answer to the Evangelical Catechism:

Question: What does our communion daily require of us?

Answer: ... being reclaimed by our Saviour and Redeemer we should live, suffer and die to his honor, so that at all times and especially in the hour of death we may cheerfully and confidently say:

Lord Jesus, for thee I live, for thee I suffer, for thee I die! Lord Jesus, thine will I be in life and death! Grant me, O Lord, eternal salvation! Amen.

The direct address to "our Saviour and Redeemer" suggests the innocence of this pietism.

trusting faith, is addressed by the revelatory text—not in predictable ways but in ways that surprise and subvert and enliven. But, then, that is what one must expect from a text that bears witness to the God who judges and restores Israel, who shows up as Friday absence and as Sunday newness. The church, when it answers to this text, is indeed called to an alternative life in the world. The world around us—with its immense power and knowledge—intends none of the vulnerability of Friday. With its capacity for control and prediction, it intends none of the surprise of Sunday. But the church, when it responds in alternative imagination, is exactly a practice of vulnerability and surprise that keeps our common life human. That is the passion that propels my exposition. In doing so, I "imagine" that we may follow "the Basel men" of the *Kirchenverein* who took the gracefulness of the Reformation with simple, joyous seriousness.

In my evangelical tradition, it is the practice of the pastor at confirmation to give each confirmand a "confirmation verse" from Scripture that was taken to be the epitome of faith for that person. When I was thirteen and confirmed by my father in St. Paul's Church, the verse he assigned me with the laying on of hands was Psalm 119:105:

> Your word is a lamp to my feet
>
>> and a light to my path.

My father, in selecting that verse for me, was of course not prescient. In the end, he had it right for me. "Your word" in the verse refers to Scripture or, more specifically, to the Torah. The Psalm affirms that Torah, the most authoritative teaching tradition of Judaism, is *the lamp and light* for the course of life. The "path" is the journey of obedience that we walk, at best, tentatively. In the fairly repetitive rhetoric of Psalm 119 there is nothing especially noteworthy about the verse. In contemporary context the claim of the verse is a blockbuster. It asserts, in the midst of many competing claims, that it is this Torah tradition of alternative that shows us how to live well. In context I understand that affirmation to be a recognition that neither the 'light" of authoritarian religion nor the "lamp" of technological secularism can finally lead to life. It is an odd claim that Jews characteristically make, a Jewish claim that is echoed and affirmed by Christians. As much as I have been intentional in my work, it is an attempt to practice that conviction. I understand that such a scholarly interpretive task is best done in an "irenic" way, capable of learning from the most impassioned critics and the most resolved canonists, without needing to dispute those who see and know differently. The governing mantra of the *Kirchenverein* pertains even to that expository task:

> In essentials unity,
>
> In nonessentials freedom,
>
> In all things charity.[29]

In biblical exposition, the "essential" is to keep an eye on the lead Character who astonishes us by showing up variously as compassionate and/or violent. In biblical exposition, the "nonessential" as a zone of freedom includes many methodological possibilities and hermeneutical variations that may be mutually respectful. In biblical exposition, "charity" among expositors might enhance the task, charity that is generous without compromising important claims. In these essays I indulge in reflection on my work with the hope that what I have said and written may empower and entice others to the task that is never finished, to trust the lamp, to heed the light, and to travel joyously on the path.

---

29. This formula has now been adopted in many quarters of the church that want to voice an ecumenical openness. It is rooted in early Lutheran pietism that was a seedbed of the *Kirchenverein*, a pietism that contrasted with what became hard-nosed confessional Lutheranism. My colleague, Lowell Zuck, following John T. Mc Neill, reports that the formula was used to conclude a statement in 1626 by Meldenius ("really Peter Meiderlin") addressed to the "theologians of the Augsburg Confession." Its usage there, and characteristically since, is in the interest of church union.

CHAPTER 1

Introduction: That the World May Be Redescribed

WE STUDY THE BIBLE IN THE CHURCH AND WE ARGUE ABOUT IT. WE read it in church and dutifully call it "The Word of the Lord." We respond to the reading with equal dutifulness, "Thanks be to God." But we do not reflect much on what we are doing and, I suggest, much of the time we are not attentive to the reading itself. In what follows in these essays I want to consider *what we are doing* when we read the Bible and *how we read* in order to accomplish what we think we are doing.

A Network of Symbols

The Bible is not ever read or studied in a vacuum. It is always read and studied and heard in a particular social context and in a particular cultural environment that teems with symbolization. The package of dominant symbols that define the social, cultural context of Bible reading we may call a "world," if we understand that "world" means a network of symbols and gestures that order and legitimate social power in a particular way.

We may take it as a fact that a "world" as a network of symbols is not a "given," but it is always a carefully constructed social fabric that intends to shape and exhibit social reality in one way rather than in many other ways that are available.[1] Thus a dominant "world" is an intentional advocacy that establishes assumptions, procedures, and goals for the manage-

---

1. The critical conviction that the social world is supple and changeable has been decisively articulated by Karl Marx; from Marx comes a continuing trajectory of critical thought that, in our time, features Michel Foucault. That contemporary critical conviction has rootage and antecedent in the ancient Scriptures of Israel.

ment of social power. Peter Berger and Thomas Luckmann have rightly spoken of "the social construction of reality," for they, like every other social scientist, are acutely aware that what is easily taken as a given is in fact a construction, even if persuasively done, even if accomplished surreptitiously.[2] In the ancient world of the Bible, the dominant life-world was constructed and managed from centers of royal imperial power or from centers of tribal authority. In each case the center of power created a fabric of narrative memory that offered a viable tradition and identification that made it possible for people to place themselves in a legitimate social environment. The great centers of socioeconomic, political, and military power depend upon the *great temple liturgies* that enacted *deeply rooted myths* to create and manage social reality.[3] We may take it that the Jerusalem establishment of David and Solomon are a pale but intentional reflection of the great practice of liturgy-myth that offered a world that certified Jerusalem power and the creator God YHWH who legitimated that urban power. As counteroffer, the tradition of the Mosaic covenant at Sinai provided an alternative grounding with a more radical social ethic rooted in the will of YHWH, the steadfast God of covenant.[4] These two offers of a "world" of YHWH lived in some tension with each other, the Jerusalem offer of coherence and security, the Sinai offer of neighborly obedience. The text, in its canonical, liturgical, storytelling practice created and continues to create a life-world that places YHWH as the key character in that imagined world.

Intentional Advocacy

As the ancient world was constituted with intentional advocacy, so our contemporary world is likewise constructed with intentional advocacy. While we may differ on detail and nuance, the main lines of that construction seem obvious. We in the United States live in a world that champions

2. Berger and Luckmann, *The Social Construction of Reality*.

3. In a previous generation, a great deal of energy was utilized in the study of the great myths of the states that were enacted through liturgy to arrange and legitimate social power. See the defining essays edited by S. H. Hooke, *Myth and Ritual*; and idem., *Myth, Ritual, and Kingship*.

4. Levenson has considered the way in which these two traditions exhibit tension with each other and yet are held together in an interpretive coherence in ancient Israel (*Sinai and Zion*).

U.S. exceptionalism.[5] From that it follows that the United States, as the last superpower, does good in the world, so that its military adventurism is for the advancement of freedom. That military adventurism which amounts to nothing less than a National Security State is in the service of controlling the global economy in order to supply unlimited consumer goods in a culture of insatiable luxury.[6] That world is constructed through government propaganda, market advertising, and technological manipulation that seek to contain and preempt all questions of "value." This constructed world is a delicate combination of aggressive secular cynicism, coupled with a veneer of religious legitimacy, so that *raw power* is nicely matched to *passionate religious conviction*.[7] In this socially constructed world, the great gaps between rich and poor and the institutional maintenance of injustice are kept carefully hidden and off the public agenda by mantras about "opportunity" and "freedom." In recent time we have recovered a great deal of data about the enslaving force of racial, ethnic, sexual violence that has remained hidden in the maintenance of a privileged socioeconomic hegemony. And most recently, the failure of both an independent judiciary and a critical press has caused this dominant construal of reality to go unchecked and unchallenged.

This world may be delineated as a ruthless savage contest for control that works violence beneath the surface of democratic mantras and religious legitimation. Thus the dominant description of reality lives at some distance from the facts on the ground. It is in that cultural milieu that the contemporary church in the United States reads Scripture. It is in that environment that the pastor says, "The Word of the Lord," and the congregation responds, "Thanks be to God." The study and reading and hearing of Scripture go on among both the victims of that demanding life-world and the beneficiaries of that life-world. And we are left to ask, What are we doing when we read Scripture?

---

5. On the current ideological utilization of the notion of U.S. exceptionalism, see Dorrien, "Consolidating the Empire."

6. See the restrained but shameless exposition of such U.S. entitlement in Joffe, *Ueberpower: The Imperial Temptation of America.*

7. See the critical exposé of this combination by Phillips, *American Theocracy*; and Johnson, *Blowback.*

Subversion and Sub-version

I propose that what we are doing in Scripture study, reading, and hearing is that we are *redescribing the world*, that is, constructing it alternatively.[8] The *"re"* in "redescription" means that the church is restless with the current, dominant description of reality because that description does not square with the facts on the ground. Thus every time the church takes up Scripture, it undertakes a serious challenge to dominant characterizations of our social world. It dares to propose an alternative reading of the world, an alternative version that is in fact a sub-version that rests beneath the dominant version in a less aggressive mode.[9] That alternative reading of reality—alternative version, "sub" version—by its very nature, intends to *subvert* dominant readings of reality. That redescription subverts the dominant description of reality on three grounds.

First, Scripture intends to call things by their right names (see Isa 5:20). While Scripture has its own share of ideological distortion, it is not committed to any of our current distortions, not beguiled by any of our propaganda, not taken in by any of our current euphemisms.[10] It is true that the church has its own long history of beguilement and its long tradition of biblical interpretation whereby we have signed on for the beguilements. But in principle the Bible is a book that invites truth-telling. Nowhere is this clearer than in the prophetic poetry that is unimpressed with dominant modes of power. But the prophetic poetry, the most evident form of sub-version, is not isolated in Scripture, but has allies in the Torah commandments, in the wisdom teaching, and in the Psalms of lament. All these texts move against conventional certitudes and become advocates for transformation. Consequently, they functioned as exposés of failed worlds. One cannot read or hear such texts without having some immediate sense that these texts that redescribe the ancient world in which they were first uttered, at the same time redescribe the world in

---

8. The theme of "redescribing" is appropriated from Ricoeur, "Biblical Hermeneutics," 31 and passim, who in turn cites Mary Hesse; see my exposition of the notion in *The Word that Redescribes the World*, 3–19 and passim.

9. See Brueggemann, "Preaching as Subversion."

10. Lifton has shown the way in which toxic euphemisms were at the heart of the conduct of the death camps (*The Nazi Doctors*, 202 and passim); see also idem, *Home from the War*. The cases Lifton cites are fairly typical of the linguistic deceptions essential to the great, brutal powers of war.

which we listen. Scripture alerts us to the awareness that the world is not as it is said to be. The reading of Scripture as redescription is a summons to re-see the world faithfully and honestly, and so to disengage from consensus-distorted description.

Second, Scripture sees worldly data within a very different frame of reference; as a result the data is interpreted differently. When the human data of society is read through the lens of market ideology, what happens is that "people" disappear into profit margins, market development, and stock options. But of course Scripture refuses such interpretive reductions. When one reads the same social data in a framework of the neighborly Torah of Sinai, then amid economic development, military adventurism, and an abundance of commodity goods, one sees neighbors who are exploited and devalued. The redescription of reality offered by the Bible retains the sense that the world community of human persons—as well as trees and squirrels and radishes and whales—constitute a community of solidarity and shared responsibility. Once that frame of reference is recognized, the data of the world must, perforce, be engaged differently.

But after calling things by their right names and paying attention to an alternative frame of reference, a third way through which the Bible redescribes the world is by reference to YHWH, the key character in the history of the world and the creator of heaven and earth to whom all creatures owe glad, doxological obedience. The centrality of the character of YHWH in this text is the defining "strangeness" of the text, a "strangeness" that cannot be erased either through the rationality of historical criticism or through the excessive certitude of confessionalism.[11] YHWH is given in this text as a live, free, unencumbered agent of newness with whom all creatures—Israel, nations, human persons, and nonhuman creatures—must come to terms.[12] In this text, everything and everyone else is rendered penultimate in the presence of this non-negotiable character.

When the church studies, speaks, and hears Scripture, it is engaged in a redescription of the world:

---

11. I use the term "strange" in the way intended by Karl Barth in his classic article, "The Strange New World within the Bible." Barth means that the Bible will not fit into any of our interpretive categories because it declares a different word for a different world.

12. On this inventory of God's "partners," see Brueggemann, *Theology of the Old Testament*, 413–564.

- one that refuses obfuscation by naming things properly in truth-telling;

- one that refuses accommodation to the seductions of power and greed by framing reality in covenantal modes; and

- one that refuses to settle for the arrogance or despair of the human project by reference to YHWH, who makes every human seduction to arrogance or despair penultimate.

The "big story" of redescription is about YHWH who creates, judges, and recreates the world. That big story, however, is teased out in a plethora of small narratives, prophecies, proverbs, poems, and songs in many modes.[13] These cannot be forced into a single common pattern; but in their plurality and diversity they attest to the elusive character of YHWH who cannot be consigned to any of our modes of controlled description. The preacher or the teacher thus recharacterizes reality that is, on the one hand, guaranteed by the freedom of this character and, on the other hand, is kept open and at risk by this character.

Embracing and Practicing the Gospel

It is immediately evident that such a redescription of reality as the Bible offers is, in the practice of the church, a stark and stunning contrast to the conventional, taken-for-granted characterization of reality in our society, dominated as it is by power and entitlement. The contrast is unavoidable as this new characterization is designed as profound challenge to conventional characterization. The term that may be used for the sum of the redescription is "gospel," the declaration that because of the reality of YHWH, the world is not as we thought it was and not as it has been described to us.[14] The use of the term "gospel" in Isa 40:9; 41:27; and 52:7 is a declaration, addressed to dislocated persons from Judah in Babylon, that the geopolitical reality of the world is decisively altered by the reality of YHWH, whose presence and purpose change everything:

13. In his discussion of "testimony," Paul Ricoeur has characterized and exposited five normative genres for "the small narratives" ("Toward a Hermeneutic of the Idea of Revelation").

14. On the term "gospel" in Old Testament usage, see Brueggemann, *Biblical Perspectives on Evangelism*, chapter 1. While the language of "gospel" will strike one as narrowly "Christian," in fact the term in the Old Testament bespeaks the implosion of YHWH as a defining agent in the life and history of Israel.

Get you up to a high mountain,

> O Zion, *herald of good tidings*;

lift up your voice with strength,

> O Jerusalem, *herald of good tidings*,

> lift it up, do not fear;

say to the cities of Judah,

> "Here is your God!" (Isa 40:9)

✷   ✷   ✷

How beautiful upon the mountains

> are the feet of the messenger who announces peace,

who brings *good news*,

> who announces salvation,

> who says to Zion, "Your God reigns." (Isa 52:7)

The claim is not different in the abrupt use of the term "gospel" in Mark concerning the new reality of Jesus of Nazareth who is the Christ:

> The beginning of the *good news* of Jesus Christ, the Son of God. (Mark 1:1)

In both uses in Isaiah and Mark, the poetry and the narrative that follow the declaration line out a wholly different world that renders old descriptions of reality to be null and void. In both uses the declaration amounts to a summons to embrace and "practice" the newly declared reality in concrete and daring ways.

It will be clear that such a redescription means to join issue in sharp ways with old characterizations of reality that are now said to be passé.

The new characterization that calls things by their right names moves to shatter the old nomenclature that proceeds by euphemism to misrepresent and distort lived reality. An extreme case of such distortion through misnomer is the rhetoric utilized to characterize in false ways the death camps of German National Socialism. That extreme use is not exceptional. We may also consider the euphemisms currently in vogue to disguise the U.S. military aggression in Iraq: "harm's way," "friendly fire," "collateral damage," all uses that are designed to make the aggression appear benign. Thus "Reverend Billy" prays:

> Dear Lord,
>
> We can't believe that bombing is called security.
>
> We can't believe that monopoly is called democracy.
>
> We can't believe that gasoline prices are called foreign policy. . . .
>
> We can't believe that racism is called crime fighting!
>
> We can't believe that sweatshops are called efficiency!
>
> We can't believe that a mall is called the neighborhood! . . .
>
> We can't believe that advertising is called free speech!
>
> We can't believe that love is called for sale!
>
> We can't believe that you think there are two political parties!
>
> We can't believe that you repeat the word "democracy" like it's a
> liturgical chant from a lost religion![15]

In every phase of public life, hegemonic rule employs misnomer to disguise the use of raw power in exploitative and manipulative ways. The function of Scripture may well be to call things by their right names in order that we may be in touch with the genuine reality in which God has called us to live.

The new characterization of reality situates social relationships in a new frame of reference. While current rhetoric in a market economy defines all relationships by leverage and power—that produces winners and losers, haves and have-nots—the language of the Bible, stemming from the covenant God of Sinai, is the language of "neighbor, brother, and sister." This recharacterization of social relationships insists that all social transactions are between neighbors and that all elements of the neighborhood need to be designed to enhance those relationships. The radical teaching of the "year of release," for example, insists that even the economy must be subordinated to and pressed into the service of the social infrastructure (Deut 15:12–18).[16] Obviously such a recharacterization has important and immediate implications for social policy.

The new characterization of reality places YHWH—creator of heaven and earth, Lord and deliverer of Israel—in the center of the historical process. It is this God who gives life and who summons to obedience. It is this God who presides over the rise and fall of the nations. This rede-

---

15. Talen, *What Should I Do If Reverend Billy Is in My Store?* 93–94.

16. See Hamilton, *Social Justice and Deuteronomy*.

scription collides with the consensus descriptions of reality featured in a consumer-driven National Security State. To be sure, that latter culture has gods of cheap grace and coercive demand, but they are gods with no power to save. This contrast is immediately contemporary in its strictures against idolatry that are voiced in the redescription, because the gods of settled consensus descriptions are indeed idols without power to save:

> Our God is in the heavens;
>> he does whatever he pleases.
> Their idols are silver and gold,
>> the work of human hands.
> They have mouths, but do not speak;
>> eyes, but do not see.
> They have ears, but do not hear;
>> noses, but do not smell.
> They have hands, but do not feel;
>> feet, but do not walk;
>> they make no sound in their throats.
> Those who make them are like them;
>> so are all who trust in them. (Ps 115:3–8)[17]

Between Crisis and Obedience

On all counts this recharacterization of reality collides with, challenges, and subverts more conventional characterizations of reality. That is what makes Scripture study and proclamation so interesting, compelling, and problematic. Even in the church, the primal venue for reading the Bible as "The Word of the Lord," such an articulation of an alternative reality is sure to evoke dispute and turmoil. Indeed the study of Scripture is designed to place readers and hearers in a crisis between *the old world* that is mostly accepted without critical assessment and *the new world* imagined in this text. It belongs to Bible reading to live in crisis and to spend our energy adjudicating that crisis. The bad news in such adjudication is that we

---

17. See also Isa 44:9–20; and Jer 10:1–16.

are left forever restless with the old consensus. The good news is that we now have some clarity about alternatives and choices to be made. Those choices are to be understood as the gift of God's Spirit who continues to "stir up" the church in its reading and hearing.

If it is true that a biblical redescription of reality places us in crisis, then it follows that Bible study creates, of itself, a venue for pastoral care and a matrix for missional obedience. This pastoral care consists in maintaining a safe, honest environment where the dispute between worlds can be adjudicated without shame, guilt, manipulation, or coercion. The missional obedience consists in specific actions and disciplines that live from and toward the new world offered in the gospel redescription. There is a powerful inclination among us (for liberals and for conservatives) to refuse the new world and to return to the familiarity of the old characterization. That inclination among us is a replication of the same inclination in ancient Israel to return from the demanding freedom of the wilderness to the "fleshpots" of enslaving Egypt:

> The Israelites said to them, "If only we had died by the hand of YHWH in the land of Egypt, when we sat by the fleshpots and ate our fill of bread; for you have brought us out into this wilderness to kill this whole assembly with hunger." (Exod 16:3)

*   *   *

> Then all the congregation raised a loud cry, and the people wept that night. And all the Israelites complained against Moses and Aaron; the whole congregation said to them, "Would that we had died in the land of Egypt! Or would that we had died in this wilderness! Why is YHWH bringing us into this land to fall by the sword? Our wives and our little ones will become booty; would it not be better for us to go back to Egypt?" So they said to one another, "Let us choose a captain, and go back to Egypt." (Num 14:1–4)

The practice of the recharacterization is a life or death matter. It is urgent because the old description and the new redescription offer quite different futures. Those who gather around this text are always choosing, yet again:

> See, I have set before you today life and prosperity, death and adversity. If you obey the commandments of YHWH your God that I am commanding you today, by loving YHWH your God,

walking in his ways, and observing his commandments, decrees, and ordinances, then you shall live and become numerous, and YHWH your God will bless you in the land that you are entering to possess. But if your heart turns away and you do not hear, but are led astray to bow down to other gods and serve them, I declare to you today that you shall perish; you shall not live long in the land that you are crossing the Jordan to enter and possess. I call heaven and earth to witness against you today that I have set before you life and death, blessings and curses. Choose life so that you and your descendants may live, loving YHWH your God, obeying him, and holding fast to him; for that means life to you and length of days, so that you may live in the land that YHWH swore to give to your ancestors, to Abraham, to Isaac, and to Jacob. (Deut 30:15–20)

*   *   *

Now therefore revere YHWH, and serve him in sincerity and in faithfulness; put away the gods that your ancestors served beyond the River and in Egypt, and serve YHWH. Now if you are unwilling to serve YHWH, choose this day whom you will serve, whether the gods your ancestors served in the region beyond the River or the gods of the Amorites in whose land you are living; but as for me and my household, we will serve YHWH. (Josh 24:14–15)

*   *   *

Elijah then came near to all the people, and said, "How long will you go limping with two different opinions? If YHWH is God, follow him; but if Baal, then follow him." The people did not answer him a word. (1 Kgs 18:21)

CHAPTER 2

Setting the Stage: The Church's Task of Interpretation

WHEN WE BEGIN TO THINK ABOUT A "HANDS ON" STUDY OF THE BIBLE, we do well at the outset to ponder the authority claimed for Scripture by the church. We notice at the beginning that obedient communities of faith (Christian, Jewish, Muslim) are the proper venue for Scripture interpretation, even though we may well be informed by the critical study offered by the academy.[1] While that critical study may boldly treat the Bible "like any other book," the church recognizes the peculiarity of the Bible and assigns to the Bible a special place and voice.

That recognition and assignment of a special place and voice to Scripture in the life of faith is only a beginning point. It acknowledges a long held, widely affirmed consensus about Scripture in the church; at the same time, the formula masks a host of deep problems and a complexity that admits no obvious resolution. The problematic and complexity of Scripture in the church are immediately evident when one considers the enormous range of interpretations of a biblical text that are regularly available and variously found acceptable. That range of interpretation is saturated with awareness of the context of interpretation and of vested interest that impinge powerfully upon our reading and interpretive habits.

The chapters that follow in this volume are addressed to those who are regularly and seriously engaged in Bible study in the church. This particular chapter is a bid that such a reader of these essays recognize

---

1. No one has done more to assert the church as the proper venue for Scripture study than Brevard S. Childs, whose recent death we lament. He focused on the term "Scripture" as a church word, on which see his major book, *Introduction to the Old Testament as Scripture.*

himself/herself as an *interpreter*, as one with a *responsibility* to decide, yet again, what the text may be saying to the church as God's live word, and as one with enormous *freedom* in that act of interpretation. That freedom means that the interpreter has wide latitude in "discovering" a voice in the text and in "assigning" a voice in the text. As a consequence the interpreter is inescapably "making" meaning and not just "finding" meaning, so that interpretation is an imaginative act of construction.[2] Any thought that we may present "biblical truth" without interpretation is an illusion and indicates an unfortunate deficit of self-knowledge on the part of the interpreter.

It is self-evident that interpretation of Scripture is unavoidable. David Tracy has nicely said that in order for a classic document that is timeless to be timely, it must be interpreted.[3] It is for that reason that a claim about the authority of Scripture is not the end of our trouble, but only the beginning. When we have accepted the Bible as normative, then we must ask: How? In what way? To what end? For what claim? To answer those questions, we must interpret. When we interpret we render judgments, and those judgments rarely claim universal assent. (To be sure, in the church's long history of interpretation there are interpretations, as in the great creeds, which claim such assent. But the problem is that the creeds about which there is general consensus are remote from us and in turn require interpretation.) Any serious engagement with Scripture requires interpretation. And interpretation is always inescapably advocacy about which there is dispute. The interpretation may be as explicit as exegesis and proclamation, or it may be as seemingly innocent as the selection of one text and not another (as with a lectionary committee), or a public reading that intones, inflects, and accents in certain ways. The fact of interpretation means that the Bible never fully has it own say, but is always in part acted upon by the interpreter. The Bible, in practice, is therefore open to various significations.

Interpretation is never objective but is always mediated through the voice, perceptions, hopes, fears, interests, and hurts of the interpreter and of the context of interpretation. Because interpretation is not objective, it is always partial and provisional. Every interpretation, then, must be kept open to the review of the whole church, which is pledged to listen as

2. The term *poesis* from which we derive "poetry" means to "make" or "perform." Thus interpretation is a "making" as well as a receiving.

3. Tracy, *The Analogical Imagination*.

a whole community to what God seems to be saying in Scripture. In the meantime we must have enough courage and confidence to offer an interpretation that for the moment is given as an authoritative disclosure.[4]

We see such courage and confidence in contemporary interpretation, most clearly among advocates of a liberation hermeneutic, interpretive voices of the Third World and other marginalized communities who speak from and for a certain context and interest.[5] They are voices of the poor and oppressed who read Scripture in terms of a "preferential option for the poor." These interpreters themselves readily acknowledge their own context and how it governs their interpretation. This perspective has now produced a rich trajectory of post-colonial interpretation that reflects and serves the faithful in exploited cultures in the world.[6]

As a result, we are now coming to see that Euro-American interpretation in classic historical-critical modes, offered in the academy mostly by white, established males, is also contextualized and speaks from and for a certain context and interest. This is true for those who speak through scientific methods (liberals) and for those who speak primarily out of a dogmatic tradition (conservatives). This does not mean that such interpretations are wrong or easily dismissed. It means that they must be taken for what they are, statements of advocacy. They may claim no interpretive privilege but must be held, along with other readings, in a church that seeks to be faithful and obedient.

The problem for a church that claims to be genuinely diversified and open is how to practice the normativeness of Scripture in a way that permits all serious interpretations be taken seriously. In a practice of genuine diversity all interpreters listen and submit their readings to the judgment of the whole church, without imagining ahead of time that the truth has been spoken in a single interpretive voice. Of course it is the case that every church tradition, liberal or conservative, readily imagines its own

---

4. The requirement of such courage calls to mind the dictum of Karl Barth:

As ministers we ought to speak of God. We are human, however, and so cannot speak of God. We ought not recognize both our obligation and our inability and by that very recognition give God the glory. That is our perplexity. The rest of our task fades into insignificance in comparison. (*The Word of God and the Word of Man*, 186)

5. On this hermeneutic, see the exploratory summary of Rowland and Corner, *Liberation Exegesis*.

6. See Sugurtharajah, *Postcolonial Criticism and Biblical Interpretation*; and Dube, *Postcolonial Feminist Interpretation of the Bible*.

trajectory of interpretation to be a faithful one. And because most church traditions are readily homogeneous, there is not often a voice of dissent raised against an advocacy interpretation that reflects both a local consensus of faith and a local vested interest and an ideological commitment.

Two implications flow from this problematic. First, we cannot be a faithful church if private, isolated communities of interpretation simply insist on reiterating their interpretations without the discipline and impingement of the whole church, especially without counter-interpretations from elsewhere in the church that are wrought in good faith. Second, if Scripture is normative, as the main body of the church attests, then it is likely that there is no more important work to do than serious, sustained Scripture interpretation. It behooves the church, in its various bodies of governance, worship, and mission, to provide sustained means whereby the church can do Scripture interpretation that is not simply ad hoc service to particular issues, that is not merely undisciplined ferment, and that is not simply the work of private communities who congratulate themselves on their own interpretation. When the church is genuinely ecumenical, it is required to listen to widely different voices of interpretation, thereby necessitating the modification of our own best, preferred interpretive judgments. The critical point is to remember that our preferred interpretation, even if passionately held, is provisional and penultimate. A great deal of courage is required to offer provisional and penultimate interpretation that, in the moment of offer, is the best reading we can imagine.

Meta-Issues

The primary work in these essays is to suggest ways to look at and ways to see when placed in front of a text. Prior to that specificity I want to identify some "meta-issues" about which a church interpreter must be aware. I believe that our awareness of these issues is more or less subliminal and not often conscious. In any case a biblical interpreter must decide—or will have decided—about these matters as they are decisive for actual textual work. I will identify two *tyrannies*, two *temptations,* and two *practical tendencies* that are likely to be faced in text study. How we posture ourselves in these matters is of great importance, even though our postures about them may have been reached not by informed study but by the slow nurture of context and experience.

Two Tyrannies

The struggle for freedom in interpretation faces *two tyrannies* that have long vexed the process of Scripture study.

Confessionalism

Along with the synagogue, the Bible has been a book that belonged to the church. In the long interpretive history of the church, the Bible, for the most part, was not taken on its own terms, but was characteristically subordinated to the primal doctrinal claims of the church. The Scripture was read in terms of "the rule of faith," the central Christological-Trinitarian convictions of the church, and was understood to be material available for the dogmatic development of faith.[7] Over time the Bible could be read so that it was subservient to the church's dogmatic tradition, without any great attention to the odd artistic attestations of the biblical text itself. The propensity to read the Bible toward the church's faith is still evident in the shape of the lectionary and in reading through "the church year," and in the more recent so-called "canonical" reading of the text. In its most extreme form this tendency has issued in "confessionalism" that allows no wiggle room for the text itself, but comes to treat the text as a closed package of settled truth.

There was, in the development of this practice, nothing intentionally sinister about the project. But it did nonetheless cause the transposition of a playful, complex, artistic text into an authoritarian enterprise that thrived on exclusionary claims that are able to sort out unambiguous truth from falsity. While mainline church practice has never fully succumbed to this tyranny, the tendency continues to be present and to surface when church interpreters are in a state of acute anxiety and are wont to "circle the wagons." It is evident in such a reading, for example in the thinness of

---

7. The "Rule of Faith," as the core theological claim of the early church, is variously understood as a cognitive representation of the Trinity and the incarnation or as a commitment to love in imitation of God's own love for the world. See Polk, *The Biblical Kierkegaard*; Peter Stuhlmacher, *How to Do Biblical Theology*; and K. E. Greene-McCreight, *Ad Litteram*.

the lectionary, that much of biblical attestation to faith is omitted in the practice of the church.

In the intellectual and cultural ferment of the sixteenth century, great effort was expended to free the Bible from that church tyranny. On the one hand, the Reformation of the sixteenth century was an insistence that the biblical text be taken for its own testimony, free from the interpretive monopoly of the church's magisterium. In fact the great Reformers did not move very far away from the dogmatic tradition of the church; but the emancipatory project was put in motion. On the other hand, along with the impetus of the Reformers, the rise of historical criticism was an attempt to read the Bible "honestly" without submission to the formal church conviction. It is not often enough recognized that historical criticism was intended to "thaw" the text away from the frozenness of church authoritarianism. This effort at emancipated reading was largely an academic one that insisted that Scripture must be subjected to critical reason as would any other book. The antidote to authoritarian absolutism was taken to be an historical approach whereby every text and textual claim was understood in terms of its origin and development, origin and development understood as relativising away from absolutism. This undertaking offered reading apart from (or even against) the church's tradition, as is evident in the contemporary work of the so-called "minimalists" in Old Testament studies and the Jesus Seminar in New Testament studies, both of which regard conventional reading in the church as distortion of the text.[8] Both contemporary enterprises take an aggressively historical approach to the text.

Reductionism

But the rise of historical criticism in turn produced its own *tyranny of reductionism* that I term "the tyranny of the academy." In practice, mainline church interpretation has committed to historical-critical study so that much that is "odd" in the text is explained away, and serious faith claims are relativized or dismissed. Historical criticism has functioned to overcome the intellectual scandal of the text that attested the unfettered

---

8. Among the prominent so-called minimalists in Old Testament studies are Niels Peter Lemche, Thomas L. Thompson, Keith Whitelam, and Philip R. Davies. Concerning New Testament study, notice may be taken of the work of Robert W. Funk and, more prominently, John Dominic Crossan and Marcus Borg.

freedom of God, the stunning energy of God's miraculous presence in the world, and revolutionary ethic that is an embarrassment to a managed world. In the end this read of the Bible is congenial to "the cultured despisers of religion," but without the evangelical impetus to subvert the modern world of Enlightenment rationality.

This second tyranny is much more prevalent in mainline churches because seminary instruction has been completely committed to historical-critical interpretation. The outcome has been an innocuous Bible that has mediated very little transformative energy in the church and that in fact is not very interesting. Such interpretation lacks compelling interest because what is centrally interesting in the biblical text is this God who stalks the earth in ways that do not accommodate modern rationality. When that God is toned down to manageable proportion, there is not much left that interests or compels.

These two tyrannies of church and academy seem to permeate all of our attempts to read the biblical text faithfully. Both "literalists" and "liberals" are beset by these tyrannies, in both cases seeking to reduce the power and elusiveness of the text to controllable dimension, both pretending not to know in advance what the text, as live word, will say.

Two Temptations

There are *two pervasive temptations* in the church concerning the Bible.

Privatization

The first is a temptation to *privatize* the Bible so that it is taken as a resource and guide for personal life to the disregard of the powerful communal dimensions of the text. This temptation is fed by a theological assumption that grows out of an old sacramentalism and a thin notion of "justification by grace," as though the Bible were all about "me and Jesus." While the temptation has arisen from doubtful theological rootage, its contemporary form is an accent on "spirituality" of a certain kind that is congenial to a "therapeutic culture." Given such a cultural assumption and given such a yearning that is a protest against the profaning materialism of our society, the Bible is read as a resource for one's comfort and well-being. We have in recent time been through a binge of reading the

Bible through a collage of preferred psychological theories that well serve a culture of "self-realization."

Perhaps an even more insidious form of distortion in Bible reading is with reference to the social agenda of the religious right that reduces the Bible to "family values," personal virtues, and moral norms, to the neglect of the socioeconomic, political implications that concern our life in the world and that centrally occupy biblical texts. Such an approach to the Bible disregards the public character of biblical faith and the way in which public, communal questions are everywhere at issue in the text. This temptation neglects the core biblical claim that the God of "personal salvation" is also the ruler of the nations. The outcome is a neglect of the transcendent sovereignty of God, but it is also neglect of the sociopolitical dimensions of human life through which we are, willy-nilly, engaged in public issues of power. Over time this approach to the Bible has so skewed the scope of the Bible that many in the church are scandalized when it is suggested that the Bible lives at the interface of the great issues of war and peace, health care delivery, economic justice, and management of the creaturely environment. When that contested public space is given up, the discourse of the church withers to safe, personal, interpersonal subjects that align the Bible in a vote for the status quo.

Politicization

The alternative temptation, featured in more "progressive" venues, is the temptation to *politicization* of the text. In this perspective everything is read as a mandate to social action and social transformation with reference to urgent contemporary issues. It cannot, of course, be denied that the Bible is largely concerned with public issues of peace and justice. Given this temptation, it is quite easy to see that the biblical text may be put of manageable use in two ways, both of which fail to recognize that our "progressive" interpretive propensity is at best penultimate. On the one hand, there is a temptation in progressive circles of interpretation to make a quite easy and uncritical move from the text to contemporary questions, while hiding or denying the complex interpretive maneuver that makes the connection possible. This is, in my judgment, variously the case with reference to welfare and disarmament, as it is with reference to abortion and homosexuality. Such interpretive connections, whether made by radicals or by reactionaries, tend to disregard the differences in the ambience of ethical issues, choices, and strategies in the ancient text and in the contemporary world. Every such advocacy is tempted too easily to make these connections and claim for itself the "obvious" endorsement of Scripture.

On the other hand, such politicization of the text runs the risk of denying the transcendent mystery of God and the eschatological claim of the text. Thus the core biblical metaphor of "Kingdom of God" cannot be immediately equated with any social construct we may have devised. The temptation moves in the direction of idolatry that wants to regard one's own political advocacy as an ultimate expression of biblical intentionality. Such politicization of the text, from any ideological perspective, requires a heavy dose of humility and a readiness to imagine that the God of the Bible may withhold full endorsement of any of our preferred options. To be sure, faithful Bible reading requires public action in the world; but such public action cannot, in my judgment, claim the God of Scripture as a fully committed partner in any of our projects.

Two Tendencies

There are, in church interpretation, two quite practical tendencies that live in profound tension with each other. These are the tendency to read the Bible in terms of *equilibrium* or in terms of *transformation*.[9] The recognition of these propensities requires from the interpreter a great deal of self-knowledge, an acknowledgment of one's readiness to tilt in one direction or the other. Both tendencies are readily found in the text itself and require ongoing adjudication without a final settlement in one direction or the other.

Equilibrium

The tendency in the Bible toward *equilibrium* can be found variously in the creation narrative, in the wisdom traditions, and most poignantly in the Priestly instructions. This tendency places the accent on order, au-

---

9. In the classic tradition of sociology, these trajectories are articulated respectively by Karl Marx and Emile Durkheim, the latter given voice in U.S. sociology by Talcott Parsons. Along with other scholars, I have suggested that the same interface operates in the Old Testament text. Indeed, this interface is at the heart of current interpretive struggles in the U.S. church; see "Trajectories in Old Testament Literature and the Sociology of Ancient Israel."

thority, discipline, and purity, all of which are seen in the Bible to be gifts and expectations of God. Elsewhere I have termed this propensity, "The legitimation of structure," a readiness to celebrate and enhance present power arrangements and present economic distribution, and to generate rationales for the maintenance of the way things are.[10] This biblical tradition is no doubt generated by those who enjoy the status quo; for good reason it is not surprising that these same traditions appeal in contemporary reading to those who favor the status quo and who regard change as loss and disintegration. It needs to be understood, with reference to this propensity, that even if these traditions cast the maintenance of the present order with reference to God, this advocacy is not innocent of sociopolitical dimensions.

Transformation

The inclination in the Bible toward *transformation* is readily found in a variety of texts, in the promise to the ancestors to go elsewhere, in the exodus narrative and its revolutionary departure from the empire, in the prophetic texts of judgment and hope. These textual traditions affirm that God stands over against present worldly arrangements and assures the rise and fall of great power. God has an intention that the world should be organized differently; God recruits a community to be engaged in a move toward the newness that God wills. This propensity emphasizes liberation, distributive justice, and the gift of freedom out beyond conventional social habits. I have termed this inclination, "the embrace of pain," by which I suggest that these texts reflect a deep awareness of the suffering caused by present arrangements and the conviction that God wills other for the world.[11] In this perspective what is lost in a move of transformation is viewed as "good riddance." It needs to be understood, with reference to this perspective, that even if these traditions cast social transformation with reference to God, this advocacy is not innocent of sociopolitical dimension.

Both of these perspectives have ample warrant in biblical texts. It is this strange bifocal character of biblical testimony that Abraham Lincoln caught so well in his Second Inaugural Address:

10. Brueggemann, "A Shape of Old Testament Theology, I: Structure Legitimation."

11. Ibid., 22–44.

Each looked for an easier triumph, and a result less fundamental and astounding. Both read the same Bible, and pray to the same God; and each invokes His aid against the other. It may seem strange that any men should dare to ask a just God's assistance in wringing their bread from the sweat of other men's faces; but let us judge not that we be not judged. The prayers of both could not be answered; that of neither has been answered fully. The Almighty has His own purposes.[12]

Indeed, eleven days after his address, he wrote to Thurlow Weed:

Every one likes a compliment. Thank you for yours on my little notification speech, and on the recent Inaugeral [sic] Address. I expect the latter to wear as well as—perhaps better than—anything I have produced; but I believe it is not immediately popular. Men are not flattered by being shown that there has been a difference of purpose between the Almighty and them. To deny it in this case is to deny that there is a God governing the world. It is a truth which I thought needed to be told; and as whatever of humiliation there is in it, falls most directly on myself, I thought others might afford for me to tell it. Yours truly.[13]

There is enough in the Bible so that every interpreter on the spectrum of stability and change can find textual support. Faithful interpretation, beyond the passion of ideological commitment, may be required to recognize and take seriously that neither the text nor the God of the text will fully echo or sign on for any particular interpretation bent in either direction.

The result is that our appropriation of scriptural texts is always and inescapably contextual and contested. Faithful reading requires a full recognition of the complexity of the text and an equally full recognition of the complexity of social reality in the midst of which we do our interpretation. In fact none of us is fully consistent about such matters because we do not everywhere, in life or in our reading horizon, come down on the side of "law and order" or on the side of emancipated newness. Nor does the biblical text!

In any interpretive community, then, what is required is contextual adjudication between these tendencies, so that both kinds of interpretation may be taken seriously. In any interpretive community where one

12. Lincoln, "Second Inaugural Address," 687.
13. Abraham Lincoln, "To Thurlow Weed," 689.

side is so powerful and decisive that the other propensity is silenced or excluded, I suggest that the community is on its way to becoming a sect that has forgotten its role as a faithful interpreter. This necessary adjudication is not the same as settlement for the lowest common denominator, but it is a resolve to entertain "the whole counsel of God" that is always thicker and more complex than our immediate social interest or moral passion.

I cite one case of twinned contemporary issues that are currently central to the matter of equilibrium and transformation, namely, the great interface of the issues of sexuality and money. That these two issues currently occupy the church is not surprising, as conservatives in the church focus on sexuality and dimensions of fidelity and liberals focus on money and dimensions of justice. The Bible affirms (a) that sexuality and money are the two great human issues through which we signal and act out power and fidelity, (b) that these two issues must be submitted to God's rule that is marked by starchy insistence and gracious generosity, and (c) that the two issues are inextricably related to each other and cannot be separated from each other as exhibits of power and fidelity.[14] Sexuality and money are of a piece as gifts of God and means of human domination and human possibility. It strikes me as a telling epitome of that interrelatedness that in the three ethical summaries of Ezekiel 18, the characterization of "righteousness" concerns (a) idolatry and the worship of the true God, (b) sexual relations in the community and (c) neighborly transactions about money:

> If a man is righteous and does what is lawful and right—if he does not eat upon the mountains or lift up his eyes to the idols of the house of Israel, does not defile his neighbor's wife or approach a woman during her menstrual period, does not oppress anyone, but restores to the debtor his pledge, commits no robbery, gives his bread to the hungry and covers the naked with a garment, does not take advance or accrued interest, withholds his hand from iniquity, executes true justice between contending parties, follows my statutes, and is careful to observe my ordinances, acting faithfully—such a one is righteous; he shall surely live, says the Lord GOD. (Ezek 18:5–9; see also vv. 10–13, 14–18; and Job 31:1, 9, 16, 24)

14. In the critical tradition, Marx and Freud, respectively, have shown how money and sexuality are primal arenas for human self-deception. The Frankfurt School, and especially Erich Fromm, has worked at holding together the insights of Marx and Freud concerning the exercise of power in these zones of human life.

Conservative interpretive voices currently focus on sexuality and advocate for social equilibrium in order to maintain social relationships, as they have been in the past; such voices tend to be silent on matters of money and the economy. Conversely, liberal interpretive voices currently focus on money and advocate social transformation as concerns health and education in order to create a new set of social relationships; such voices tend to disregard much of the text concerning sexuality. There is no easy or obvious way through the current dispute. But a beginning point may be that the church should not speak or teach on either of these issues without a complementary statement about the other. That is, that conservatives not make sexuality "the issue," and liberals not make economics "the issue," but all the advocates and the biblical interpreters behind them may stand together in modesty before the rule of God who renders all of our passions and fears and hopes to be penultimate. While God may "will one thing," it is clear that the complex process of interpretation of the Bible is not able to will one thing. Serious Bible reading may well recognize that there are voices in the text that are other than echoes of our own voices. The largeness of God's will and hope for the world certainly cannot be reduced to or contained in our best interpretive inclinations.

It is evident that biblical interpretation is exceedingly problematic. I have identified three aspects of that problematic:

1. The tyrannies of reductionism (in the church) and dismissiveness (in the academy).

2. The temptation to privatize the text and the temptation to politicize the text, on the assumption that we know what the text will say before we listen.

3. The practical tendencies to equilibrium and to transformation, without pausing to heed voices other than our own.

Faithful Interpretation

The following essays operate from a very high commitment to the authority of Scripture. But formulations of the authority of Scripture are empty mantras until we get down to specific texts. And then it is apparent that issues of authority are transposed into issues of interpretation. It is precisely how authority results in interpretation that is our vexed question. An authoritative Bible that is not the subject of faithful interpretation has little generative power or pertinence for the community of faith. Conversely, interpretation that does not grow out of a sense of authority can rush too readily to become subjective, partisan, and ideological.

In my church tradition the catechism had at its center a question about "the humiliation and exaltation of Christ" for which Phil 2:5–11 was the proposed answer.[15] In that Christological witness to the church, Paul admonishes his addressees, "Let each of you look not to our own interests, but to the interests of others" (v. 4). That, it seems to me, is the hallmark of faithful interpretation, because our interpretation is never innocent and never apart from contextual contestation.

In terms of theological rootage our interpretation is to be done in the wake of Jesus who is crucified and risen, who had nowhere to lay his head (Matt 8:20), who was friend of publicans and sinners (Luke 7:34), who became poor that by becoming poor he might make many rich (2 Cor 8:9). I submit that what we know of Jesus is a clue about interpretation. Our interpretation (which is the real practice of authority) is to be crucified and risen to new truthfulness.[16] Our interpretation is not to be done in our comfortable established posture, but as exiles on the way. Our interpretation is to be amenable to the poor and marginal for whom our controlled epistemology, our assured affluence, and our certain morality lack credibility. Our interpretation is an act of our poverty and not of our fullness, so that it might enrich others.

Practically, our interpretation is to be done gathered around the Eucharistic table that is an anticipation of our gathering around the throne of mercy. In my church tradition that table is called "The Welcome Table," where all may come. Well, we never come without our interpretations. As we watch the bread broken and given to all, we are able to see that faithful interpretation does not speak the truth unless it is broken truth. As we watch the wine poured out, we know that where our lives are not poured

15. My phrasing deliberately alludes to question and answer #72 in *The Evangelical Catechism* that stands at the root of my particular pietistic theological tradition. My forebears understood that this early Christian hymn is a core statement of the "emptying" theology that is crucial for the church.

16. In his study of the theological symbol of "fatherhood," Paul Ricoeur demonstrates the way in which such a freighted symbol must be broken and then recovered for faithful usage; *The Conflict of Interpretations*, 468–97. Ricoeur's statement of such a symbol evidences the way in which "crucifixion and resurrection" belong to the core of faithful interpretation.

out, our interpretation is a lie. The interpretive language that grows from the bread broken and the wine poured out is not the language of certain scholasticism, partisan moralism, or strident revolution. We will not responsibly claim the authority of Scripture unless we recover its language that is the language of trust and amazement, gratitude and obedience. Then *the words* may match *the sacrament*!

I move from this essay to particular texts, a move that is not easy or obvious. I make that move with the question, "How shall we interpret in ways that are not enthralled to the tyrannies, reduced by the temptations, or unaware of our interpretive inclinations to either stability or transformation?" Such an unencumbered approach is never fully available; but I suggest five pointers to biblical interpretation that may have generative power in the church toward missional obedience.

1. While I have no predilection for the term "postmodern," in fact the interpretation now required in the church is interpretation that is *after modern Enlightenment rationality*, i.e., modernity. The twin perspectives of modern interpretation—historical-critical and fundamentalist—both reached beyond the text itself to other modes of certainty, either critical or confessional. Interpretation that may be conveniently termed "postmodern," or better, post-foundational or post-liberal recognizes that there is no governing certitude in interpretation, no ultimate "final solution" to the text, because it is a living text that testifies to the living God.[17] Thus faithful interpretation is always an open-ended, processive enterprise that refuses closure and that anticipates being yet again surprised, even by familiar texts. The pastoral responsibility in such interpretation is to engage the congregation in the processive task of hearing what is being said afresh to the church.

2. Such interpretation, while attentive to the specificity of the text, is indeed spirit-led. The claim that Scripture is "inspired," that is, spirit inhabited, pertains to the entire process of the formation, transmission, and interpretation of the text. The spirit is God's forceful, generative presence that repeatedly blows settled reality beyond itself, including the settled reality of the text. Such inter-

17. See Thiel, *Nonfoundationalism*; and Brueggemann, "The Re-emergence of Scripture: Post-Liberalism."

pretation may appeal to and be informed by historical criticism and be alert to confessional dimensions in the text. But when the interpreter gives herself over to the text that is spirit-inhabited, the text often yields new meanings that are in the detail of the text to which the interpreter attends.

3. Such postmodern, spirit-led interpretation is essentially an artistic engagement with the artistry of the text. By this formulation, I have two matters in mind. First, I believe that all quality artistry is inspired, so that the artist is empowered and authorized to move beyond self to receive what is given. Thus a good poet or novelist finally can only say, "words came." Or "words were given" that fit no presupposition. Such given words permit the voicing of what is not until this moment of utterance. With the endless preoccupation with historical questions that has smitten both liberal and conservative interpreters, much interpretation of Scripture has been neglectful of artistry that enacts a cunning thickness that carries its own slice of truth.

Second, by emphasis upon the artistic, I intend to juxtapose artistry with ethical dimensions of the text.[18] The church has rightly always been preoccupied with the ethical claim of the text. But that emphasis has caused much interpretation to become didactic with a ready tilt toward ideology. Good artistry is never didactic and does not seek to instruct. It intends, rather, to let us see, and then to let us respond as we will. A case in point, an obvious case in point, is Jesus' parables that seek to show rather than to instruct. Good art does not give closure, but invites those who see to probe in order to see more, to enter into the thickness and to entertain the cunning, and so to be drawn into a mode of reality that is dependent upon the detail of the artistry. Biblical texts are essentially acts of art that invite us into what cannot be captured, but only offered in glimpses and in traces. Interpreters must honor and take seriously such an offer of reality that uncloses the world for newness, that discloses what had been closed, that reveals what had

---

18. My teacher, Samuel Terrien, has shown how the "contemplative" is juxtaposed to the ethical in the Bible; *The Elusive Presence*. His book is a study of how the aesthetic in the Bible is important, even though it has most often been neglected in pursuit of the ethical.

not been seen or heard. It is this unclosing, disclosing revealing that the church has dared to name as "revelation."

4. My own way of speaking about spirit-led action with the text is to speak of the work of the text as an act of imagination and our interpretation as a derivative act of imagination.[19] By this language I mean the capacity and freedom and courage to "image" (picture) a world other than the one that appears to us as a given reality.[20] Thus it is the capacity to receive a world as "other," as a gift of God's spirit, and to live in glad obedience toward that world in disengagement from the "given" world at hand. Imaginative inter- pretation, or as I have put it, "prophetic imagination" or "hopeful imagination," is to host an alternative construal of reality that is rooted in this artistic text that refuses to conform to "common sense" analysis. It is for that reason that imaginative interpretation must be "postmodern" or "postfoundational," because it refuses to submit to such givens. Such venturesome interpretation, from the perspective of "given" rational liberalism or "given" conservative confessionalism, appears to be "wild." It is only as "wild" as the spirit that blows the text open and as wild as the artists who have made the text available to us.

5. This *post-foundational, spirit-led, artistic, imaginative* interpretation that offers a "sub-version" of reality is, in the terms of Paul Ricoeur, an act of "second naiveté."[21] By the term Ricoeur acknowledges that a first, simplistic naiveté about the text has been overcome by acute critical awareness. That is a common achievement of critical study. But the interpretation now required of us does not linger excessively over criticism, as we have been wont to do in seminary instruction. It pushes beyond it or is pushed beyond criticism by spirit-led artistry to receive a new world imagined through the text, thus "second naiveté" after criticism:

   • An interpreter in second naiveté has seen the Bible critically, but after criticism receives the Bible as a gift of God's spirit;

---

19. For one of my several efforts to articulate the importance of imagination in inter- pretation, see *Texts under Negotiation*.

20. See Searle, *The Construction of Social Reality*.

21. On Ricoeur's notion, see Wallace, *The Second Naiveté*.

- An interpreter in second naiveté has seen the self critically, but after the criticism of self takes the self as an empowered, beloved, forgiven agent of God's newness;

- An interpreter in second naiveté has seen God critically and is aware of God's violent infidelity, but after criticism takes the God given us in the Gospel as the way, the truth, and the life;

- An interpreter in second naiveté has seen the world critically, and is aware of the world as an unwelcoming place, but after criticism takes the world as a venue for the practice of God's righteousness.

The challenge of interpretation is for the church to be honest and knowing and then to commit naiveté, ready for hearing a word of life and living a life of glad obedience. The church has so much to unlearn about the Bible. It practices that unlearning and relearning one text at a time. Each time it is addressed by a text it may recognize a gracing voice and an open possibility; and so it lives in joy.

CHAPTER 3

Steps in Interpretation: Jeremiah 5:14–17 as Example

WHEN I BEGAN MY DOCTORAL WORK IN OLD TESTAMENT STUDIES FIFTY years ago, there was a consensus on the big issues of scholarship. That consensus on the *method* of historical-critical interpretation had resulted in a consensus of "assured results" of the *substance* of scholarship. There continued to be a sometimes-harsh dispute in those days between American scholars and German scholars concerning the early history of Israel.[1] But even in that dispute, there was agreement that the proper questions to ask were historical questions of two types. On the one hand, there was the question of the "historical reliability" of a biblical claim for historicity. On the other hand, there was an attempt to situate texts in proper historical contexts, so that the "author" was responding to a particular historical setting, and the interpreter could rightly judge the "authorial intention" of the text, especially when it was located in an identifiable context.

Such an assumption provided some sense of coherent certainty about the text, even though that coherence was critically informed. By and large the older communities in "mainline" seminaries proceeded on the basis of these assumptions and had considerable confidence in their results. This method was widely regarded with confidence, for it seemed clear that the approach was critical and not propelled by either theological conviction or personal preference. The method provided some ground for a remarkable claim of scholarly "objectivity" and was dominated by historical issues. Only belatedly have we been able to see that such an approach and such confidence are permeated by a quite remarkable innocence on the part of its practitioners.

1. See Bright, *Early Israel in Recent History Writing*.

Rhetoric, Art, and Imagination

When I began study at Union Theological Seminary in New York, I began my study with James Muilenburg, then the senior Old Testament teacher in the United States with a background in literary studies. Muilenburg had been quietly staking out a quite different approach to biblical texts. He was still quite committed to and informed about historical-critical studies and had done some archeological work. But his passion was for an analysis of rhetoric that, in the first instant, bracketed out historical questions and focused upon the rhetorical shape and force of the text itself. As he published a number of articles in this approach, paying very close attention to the rhetorical detail of the text, his major articulation of method and exemplar interpretation was his work on Second Isaiah in *The Interpreter's Bible*, which at the time was a rather dramatic tour de force.[2] A decade later, honored as the President of the Society of Biblical Literature, his presidential address formally traced out his method as "rhetorical criticism."[3] While rhetorical criticism came late to the study of the Old Testament text, over time it has begun to impinge upon the hegemony of historical-critical methods. While some scholars have regarded historical criticism and rhetorical criticism as an either/or, it is now commonly agreed among scholars that the matter is a both/and. Historical questions must be asked; it is increasingly clear that historical questions do not take us very far and we finally must attend to the text itself.

My own approach to interpretation is very much in the tradition of rhetorical criticism, and, as I get older, I have become increasingly aware of how much I am influenced and shaped by Muilenburg. Since his presidential proposal in 1969, it is fair to say that many scholars have taken up the work of rhetorical criticism so that it enjoys widespread usage as an acceptable method of interpretation.[4] That perspective was given major impetus by Robert Alter in his influential books, *The Art of Biblical Narrative* and *The Art of Biblical Poetry*.[5] It is instructive that in the titles of both books Alter uses the term "art." Such a suggestive usage is a clue

2. Muilenburg, "The Book of Isaiah, Chapters 40–66."

3. Muilenburg, "Form Criticism and Beyond."

4. The most faithful practitioner of Muilenburg's program is Phyllis Trible; see her most valuable introduction to the method, *Rhetorical Criticism*.

5. Alter, *The Art of Biblical Narrative*; and *The Art of Biblical Poetry*.

to an interpretive perspective that is in tension with the more "scientific" perspective of historical criticism.

The recognition that the texts themselves are artistic exhibits and that interpretation, in its turn, is an artistic enterprise has pushed interpretation in new directions. The accent on the "artistic" means that interpretation will never satisfy a "scientific" hope for precision; nor will it ever meet the hope of theological "absolutism" that wants texts to yield unambiguous certitudes. An artistic approach recognizes that the text must be honored in its cunning complexity and not reduced to a single thin outcome. This approach requires a good bit of imagination that, at its best, is resonant with the imagination of those who initiated, transmitted, and treasured the text. The sense of both the text and the interpreter as acts of imagination enables one to see how the world (and God) may be delineated if we follow the lead of the rhetoric of the text.[6] This means that interpretive outcomes will be tentative, because new interpretations will always yield rich and suggestive outcomes. (It is to be recognized that our best "reads" of reality—political, scientific, or whatever—are to some great extent acts of imagination, even if those acts are informed by and called to account by "the facts on the ground," because even "the facts on the ground" are in some measure outcomes of imagination.)

Thus I conclude that our interpretive enterprise—conducted in either a religious or an academic venue—is the work of a community of imagination that is, in general, agreed about responsible method, but is nonetheless engaged in imagination. Such a way of understanding the interpretive task goes well beyond anything that Muilenburg proposed; it is not difficult to see that such awarenesses were inchoately present in his perspective. It is evident, moreover, that our common self-awareness about the interpretive task has moved well beyond the older effort at "objective work." Such a movement in interpretation follows the general intellectual climate of Western culture that has moved, willy-nilly, beyond scientism and objectivism and positivism that invites to a "thickness" that opposes many thin certitudes.[7]

6. The point is nicely articulated in the title of the book, *Preaching the Sermon on the Mount: The World It Imagines*, edited by David Fleer and Dave Bland. The dare of this fine collection of sermons and essays is the question, "Dare we live in the world imagined in the Sermon on the Mount?" Thus such imagination is a quite practical summons to an alternative life.

7. The notion of "thickness" came from the work of Gilbert Ryle and was given broad

This movement toward the artistic in interpretation is perhaps nicely evidenced in the interpretive work of Gerhard von Rad, arguably the most important Old Testament interpreter of the twentieth century. Von Rad was thoroughly grounded in the erudition of German historical criticism. He himself was an artistic force, and so he moved beyond the critical categories he had inherited to engage in theological interpretation of a most imaginative kind. In one paragraph he reflects on the textual *minimums* that are acceptable to historical criticism and the theological *maximums* that are offered in the text itself and that are the work of ongoing interpretation.[8] The interface and struggle between such minimums and maximums is both an arena of dispute and a venue for generativity. The more one fears interpretive absolutism from "theological types," the more one becomes "a minimalist." Conversely, the more one is open to theological interpretation and the thickness of meaning proposed by the text, the more one is driven to "the maximum." The uneasy relationship of academy and church in the United States is exactly a rendition of this ten-

---

currency by Clifford Geertz. It has entered into theological discourse primarily through the work of George Lindbeck, *The Nature of Doctrine*, 113–24.

8. Von Rad, *Old Testament Theology*, 1:108: "Historical investigation searches for a critically assured minimum—the kerygmatic picture tends toward a theological maximum." His further exposition of the point is as follows:

> Thus there is a clear tension between the account actually given in the narrative and the intention of the narrator, whose aim was, with the help of this material, to describe the conquest of the land by all Israel, and who, in so doing, asked too much of it. In the end this conception was most succinctly given in the narrator's words that under Joshua Israel took possession of the whole land "at one time" (אֶחָד פַּעַם Josh.x.42). This was the rounding off of the construction of that magnificent picture made by later Israel of Jahweh's final saving act. Beyond it no further unification was really any longer possible. But our final comment on it should not be that it is obviously an "unhistorical" picture, because what is in question here is a picture fashioned throughout by faith. Unlike any ordinary historical document, it does not have its centre in itself; it is intended to tell the beholder about Jahweh, that is, how Jahweh led his people and got himself glory. In Jahweh's eyes Israel is always a unity: his control of history was no improvisation made up of disconnected events: in the saving history he always deals with all Israel. This picture makes a formidable claim, and actually in the subsequent period it proved to have incalculable power to stamp affairs. How this came about is quite interesting. Israel made a picture of Jahweh's control of history on his people's behalf whose magnificence far surpasses anything that older and more realistic accounts offered. Faith had so mastered the material that the history could be seen from within, from the angle of faith. What supports and shapes this late picture of Israel's taking possession of the land is a mighty zeal for and glorification of the acts of Jahweh. (Ibid., 302)

sion. The interplay of the scientific and the artistic is, I believe, inescapably dialectical. When the artistic drifts toward absolutism—as is often done in church interpretation—then the work of the academic and the scientific is evoked to prominence. When the academic and scientific work becomes excessively arid—as it tends to become—there is a "yearning for meaning" that evokes artistic, imaginative interpretation.

My own work has been situated in this interface. While I have been deeply informed by historical scholarship, I have not found it to be particularly interesting or generative for myself, and so have focused on the artistic and the imaginative. My own social location in a church seminary and a larger church constituency has no doubt been formative for my stance of interpretation. In what follows, I will trace out with some practicality what I have learned about interpretive method that is situated in an artistic trajectory of Muilenburg.

Three Steps

Over my years of teaching I have continued to reflect on steps in textual interpretation that can be done, so to speak, "on the run." I am familiar with the usual menu of "exegetical steps" that are long and complicated, and have offered a few such directives myself. But I am aware that for most church interpreters, preachers and teachers, such a menu is wholly unrealistic and likely will be treated only with neglect. I do not want at all to encourage neglect of texts, nor dumbing down so that texts are not in fact studied at all. But I believe that a less complicated procedure is of some value, because even busy people can "read while they run" (Hab 2:2). To that end, I have proposed and taught a relatively simple practice of interpretation in three steps.

Prior to those three steps that I will delineate in some detail, I mention two other matters that concern textual interpreters. First, Scripture scholars are preoccupied with "getting the text right," and so engaging in textual criticism. While this is an important matter, most serious readers of the Bible are not competent to engage in textual criticism, for it is a highly technical matter. While there are occasionally textual issues that need to be adjudicated, for most readers the best procedure is to find a good, reliable translation and to stick with it. Where there is a textual matter of great import, consultation with a critical commentary is the best resource.

Second, historical criticism has taught us that texts must be read in context, and not as timeless statements in a vacuum. The recovery of Israel's history has provided great illumination of the context in which texts were perhaps initially formed. Except that the current turmoil concerning the history of ancient Israel suggests that we know much less than we thought about historical context in ancient Israel. While we may wish to make much more specific the context of texts (and should when we are able to), it is sufficient (and often only possible) to situate a text rightly in a great period of Israel's history—pre-monarchal, exilic, or post-exilic. Or if we wish to take an approach that is "emic," we may take the context in which Israel purportedly places the text, as long as we know what we are doing.[9] Contextual study can take us only so far, for we need not linger except to see that a general context can yield a certain angle of vision for reading the text.

With the rise of so-called "canonical criticism," we are alert to the possibility that the important context for a text is its placement in the literature (that is, not in history), so we may ask where a text is located within its own "book," or more broadly, in Scripture generally.[10] Attention

---

9. I have taken the term "emic" from Norman Gottwald, as it refers to the self-understanding of the makers and users of the text, that is, "from the consciousness of the people in the culture being explained." Gottwald, *The Tribes of Yahweh*, 785 n. 558, nicely contrasts "emic" with "etic":

> The terms "emic" and "etic" in ethnological theory were coined by the linguist Kenneth Pike on analogy with phon*emic* and phon*etic*. "*Emics*" refers to cultural explanations that draw their criteria from the consciousness of the people in the culture being explained, so that emic statements can be verified or falsified according to their correspondence to or deviation from the understanding of the cultural actors. "*Etics*" refers to cultural explanations whose criteria derive from a body of theory and method shared in a community of scientific observers. These cultural explanations constitute "a corpus of predictions about the behavior of classes of people." Etic statements cannot be verified or falsified by what cultural actors think is true, but only by their predictive success or failure. "Emics" systematically excludes "etics," but "etics" makes room for "emics" insofar as what cultural actors think about their action is part of the data to be accounted for in developing a corpus of predictions about lawful social behavior.

10. This is the point of one aspect of what Brevard S. Childs has called "canonical criticism." This perspective is pursued in his book, *Introduction to the Old Testament as Scripture*.

to the interface of text and context is important, but it should not take too much time and energy; the really important matter is the text itself.

Focus on the specific text need not be without intentional discipline, nor need it be anti-intellectual or anti-critical. Such a focus on the text itself, however, is to be clearly differentiated from the older historical-critical methods; for the texts, I suggest, require no learned apparatus beyond a sensibility that is alert and discerning, and which benefits from the accumulated awareness of reading large numbers of texts carefully.

Step 1: Rhetorical Analysis

The beginning point—and the step that requires the most care, time, and energy—is to do a *close reading of the rhetoric*, to go *inside* the text to see how it is put together rhetorically and how it functions with the parts serving the whole.[11] One of the failures of historical criticism is that it most often did not go "inside the text," but remained on the outside of the text, uninterested in internal dynamics. Such a stance outside the text is evident in the fact that very much historical criticism never read the text but only read *about* the text, being more interested in historical matters outside the text than in the effective function of the text per se.

When one does close reading, one attends to words, patterns, repetitions, the placement of words, and word parallels. Very often it turns out, in Hebrew rhetoric, that great rhetorical force is carried by grammatical particles (e.g., for, because, since, therefore), conjunctions (e.g., and, but, yet), and prepositions (e.g., in, by, from, to, between) that we mostly skip over when reading English translations. When doing such close reading, it is important to focus on the *rhetoric* of communication and persuasion, and not an "idea" or a "concept," a big temptation for readers with either a theological or an historical interest. The texts of the Old Testament characteristically have an affective dimension, and to look only for cognitive content will most often miss the point.

While it may appear a bit "hokey," my own recommendation is that the reading of the text should entail making a chart of the rhetoric of the text, so that one can see the interfaces and connections between words and how they play upon and against each other. Such a chart would in-

---

11. The study of the book of Jonah by Phyllis Trible, (*Rhetorical Criticism*) is the most sustained example we have of the process of going "inside the text" to sense its dynamic intentionality.

clude lines and arrows and circles that connect the terms to each other so that the rhetoric is characteristically seen not to be linear in any modern sense, but circular or spiral so that the rhetoric often returns at the end to the accents of the beginning. In doing such an analysis it is important to write down and make visible and available each repeated fragment so that there are no shortcuts, nor should summaries be permitted.

The consequence of such an exercise is: (a) to see that the text is most often an intricately crafted design of interrelated signs that compel the engagement of the reader or the listener; and (b) to see that this intricate system of signs, when taken as a whole, is an act of artistic imagination that offers to the reader—in the moment of reading—an imagined "world" that invites engagement and that most often appeals for a response or for a decision. The charting of rhetoric is open to continuing revision; the more one attends to the text, the more one may take notice of the artistic finesse that is present in the text. Engagement with that artistic finesse is characteristically generative of new insight, for the reader may be taken up in the artistic enterprise of the text.

Step 2: Key Word Analysis

A carefully drawn close reading that includes attention to repetition and linkage between words will characteristically cause certain words to surface as peculiarly important in carrying the freighted intentionality of the text. Once those words have surfaced through close reading, the second step that I suggest is an analysis of the key words. Key word analysis—for which one needs a concordance—is not designed to collect all of the other uses of the term, for such a collection of itself tells almost nothing. Rather, the purpose of key word analysis is to locate—when we can—other uses of the term in other texts that may illuminate this particular usage. My experience with key word analysis is that focus on a large quantity of parallel uses without focus on uses that will illuminate the text under study leads to much wasted effort. A proper procedure may require inquiry into many other uses of the word before we are able to identify the few uses that do in fact bear upon this present usage. When one finds a genuinely illuminating usage, then one can engage in some interpretive interplay between the two texts to great advantage.

Step 3: Social Analysis

Once the first two steps that I have suggested are completed, one is generally able to identify the intentionality of the text. The third step that I
practice and recommend is to ask what peculiar *advocacy* is underway
in this text. This step entails the assumption that every text, like every
serious literary effort, is in some sense an advocacy. This means that there
are no texts that are neutral, innocent, or disinterested. Every text may
be imagined in some kind of venue where there are other texts making
other kinds of advocacies, even if we do not immediately have that text
at hand. (An example of this is that the Book of Job cannot be read in all
of its poignancy unless one understands that the text of Proverbs is the
text with which it is interfaced, for Proverbs offers the settled world of
moral cohesiveness, the very world that Job intends to disrupt.) This third
step is, I propose, essential to any critical interpretation. It has been for
me greatly shaped by the emergence of the sociological criticism that is
especially evident in the work of Norman Gottwald. In a series of studies,
and especially in his magnum opus, Gottwald has shown that texts characteristically are engaged in an ideological advocacy for a certain kind of
Yahwism against other ideological claims.[12] From Gottwald I have learned
that every text carries with it a social intention.

This third step makes important demands of two kinds upon the
contemporary interpreter. First, it requires serious and sustained attention to the longstanding *ideological disputes* that emerged and persisted in
ancient Israel, sometimes vis-à-vis the non-Israelite neighbors and sometimes within the community of Israel. Some of the recurring struggles
were between, for example:

- Israel and Judah

- rivals for the throne

- large estate owners and peasants

- urban elites and villagers

- rival priestly groups

- supporters of YHWH and supporters of Baal

12. See Gottwald, *The Tribes of Yahweh*, 102–3, for his summary of the ideological
intentionality of the early traditions of Israel. While Gottwald's proposal has been critiqued and refined, it still stands as a major touch point in attending to the ideological
character of the text.

This is a recent emergence in scholarship that was barely on the horizon of conventional historical criticism.

Second, this step requires the interpreter to have some awareness about self and about the self's interpretive community as a community of ideological interest. That is, the grist of a textual advocacy may be uncongenial to the interpreter's intent or to the community of interpretation served or represented. Such lack of congeniality is no reason not to take the text seriously; it is to indicate that the advocacy of the text—which may be beneath the surface of the text—needs to be taken with great seriousness, whether it is congenial or not.

A comment about this third step. My experience as a teacher is that students often transpose this third step about *advocacy* into a question about *contemporary relevance*: "What is the text saying to *us*?" That is not the point of my third step. Rather, it is to try to enter into *the ancient advocacy* to see how the text sounded and felt and may have been received in that ancient community. This may require the identification of the *counter-advocacy* either as an act of imaginative conjuring or by the location of texts that take a counter position.[13] Such a question invites into the deep conflicts of the ancient community, conflicts that generated texts; by this process we are able to see what it is like to take sides in those ancient disputes. Only after we have done that to the best of our capacity can a question of contemporaneity be posed.

All of these elements of study—the *force of imagination*, the *hosting of intertextuality*, and the *pondering of ideology*—focus on the concrete text as such. Indeed, I ask my students as they focus on a particular text to entertain in a provisional way the possibility that this is the only text we have. If this were the only text we had (subjunctive, contrary to fact), what would we have disclosed of God, of world, of church, of self? The text *per se* needs, in my judgment, to be entertained in its own stark particularity before rushing to more general claims that inevitably tone down the concrete starkness. Only after such an exercise do I ask students to resituate the text in the larger scopes of canon and ongoing confessional traditions. The intention of such a strategy is to encourage the most radical non-foundational possibility, to engage the text in its particularity without reference to protective universals.

13. On counter-advocacy that challenges dominant theological claims, see Brueggemann, *Theology of the Old Testament*.

Jeremiah 5:14–17

I now turn to the poetic unit of Jer 5:14–17 as a characteristic case of what I might suggest with students—seminarians, pastors, lay people—in pursuing my simple three-step interpretive procedure.

Rhetorical Analysis

The initial "Therefore" (v. 14), in prophetic rhetoric, indicates a prophetic sentence now to be pronounced on the basis of the indictment already offered in vv. 12–13. The indictment is that Judah has declared God to be passive and irrelevant, and so has made the prophets of YHWH irrelevant as well:

> They have spoken falsely of YHWH,
>
> > and have said, "He will do nothing.
>
> No evil will come upon us,
>
> > and we shall not see sword or famine." (Jer 5:12)

The sentence of judgment in our verses is the decisive self-assertion of YHWH who, according to prophetic conviction, is never passive or irrelevant in the way in which complacent Jerusalem assumes (v. 14). The one who speaks, the "God of Hosts," is capable of two powerful "I" statements, "I am making . . . I am bringing," each introduced by the attention-getting particle "Behold" (*hinneh*). These two statements correlate with the two indictments of vv. 12–13. The God who *brings* is not passive ("will do nothing"); the prophet who *speaks* is not idle ("nothing but wind"). The prophecy of punishment contradicts and gives the lie to both preferred assumptions of an unconditional monarchy and an unqualified temple presence.

The two self-announcements of YHWH eventuate in the term "nation" that now becomes the *Leitmotif* of the poem, an aggressive, powerful, inscrutable historical-military force on the horizon of weak, helpless Judah, appearing at the behest of the self-announcing God. The term "people" (*goi*) occurs four times in v. 15, each time modified by a powerful, ominous adjective: far away, enduring, ancient, with an unrecognized language. Inserted between the first and second uses of the term "nation" is the vocative, "House of Israel," a pregnant contrast between the unnamed nation so ominous and the named House of Israel uttered without any impressive adjective, as bereft of impressive adjectives as it is of staying power.

After the double divine "I" of vv. 14–15, YHWH appears no more in the poem. Now the definitive player is the "ancient, enduring nation" who acts aggressively against the "House of Israel" at the behest of YHWH (double agency). The full attention of the listener is focused on the "nation," given a characterization of threat and awe not unlike the monsters of Joban poetry (Job 40:15–24; 41:1–34). In the face of that sure coming threat, the "House of Israel" does not *know*, does not *understand* (*shemaʿ*), that is, is a helpless recipient of the threat. Israel can make no serious response and offer no serious resistance.

Now the dominant rhetorical accent is on "they/their"—nothing of "YHWH," nothing of "House of Israel." Verse 16 characterizes massive military power, and v. 17 details the inescapable effect of that military power: They shall "eat up"—four times. The imagery is of a marauding, destroying, reckless, invading force. The four-fold verb is matched by a series of four word-pairs—harvest/food, sons/daughters, flocks/herds, vines/fig trees—that concretely characterize the rapacious action of an occupying army and that altogether amount to everything upon which the community depends—its food supply, its economy, its security, and indeed its children. The rhetorical effect of the four-fold statement is cumulative. Each word-pair intensifies the previous statement of loss, until all is lost, all is helpless, all is confiscated, all is hopeless.

After the four-fold "eat up" in v. 17, the poem turns abruptly to a different verb in v. 18 that NRSV renders "destroy" but that perhaps is better rendered "forcibly seize and occupy."[14] "Forcibly" because it is by savage sword, before which even the fortified cities of Judah are helpless because of false trust. The positioning of "trust" penultimately in the poem before the concluding "sword" is a remarkable rhetorical move, because the term "trust" reintroduces the theological dimension of allegiance to YHWH that has been absent in vv. 15–17.[15] Israel is helpless, not because of poor military preparation but because of the dismissal of YHWH in v. 12, for which it stands indicted. The term "trust" at the end of the poem is a reference to "false trust," the theological frame in which the coming military threat is to be interpreted.

14. There is a textual problem in this verse, but I have followed the conventional translation.

15. See Ps 146:3 for "trust" (*bṭḥ*) used negatively, a rebuke against false trust.

This rhetorical analysis is readily reduced to a chart so that the entire system of signs can be seen together. I regularly ask students to present such a chart that might look like this one:

Therefore (*lkn*): YHWH, God of Hosts

   Because (*yᶜn*) . . .

  Behold (*hinneh*) . . . I am making . . .

    Behold (*hinneh*) . . . I am bringing . . .

       goy from afar . . . O House of Israel . . .

       goy enduring . . .

       goy ancient . . .

       goy you do not know . . .

         you do not understand (*shemaᶜ*).

    Their quiver . . . like a tomb . . .

       mighty warriors (*gibborim*).

    They devour . . . harvest and food;

    They devour . . . sons and daughters;

    They devour . . . flocks and herds;

    They devour . . . vines and fig trees;

    They destroy (*yrš*) with a sword . . . fortified cities

       in which you trust (*bṭḥ*).

It is difficult at the outset to give students freedom to exercise their reading capacity, to assure them that there is no one right way, to permit themselves enough imaginative latitude to articulate what is seen and heard in the text. In a pedagogical situation I invite students to present, share, and comment on their charted analyses, and then to pay attention to other student presentations. In the process students begin to notice different peculiar nuances offered variously, but also the constants that recur.

The value of such an approach is to slow down to notice detail, and to sense the emotive force of utterance by imagining what it was like to *hear* the prophecy. It is the great temptation in our society—and especially in church culture that is excessively in pursuit of "certitude"—to read for "ideas" and "concepts" and "propositions." But ideas, concepts, and propositions are not very interesting, have little capacity to engage, and are not the first order of business in the rhetoric of the Old Testament. Behind idea, concept, or proposition—an endless Western preoccupation—the text is after figure, image, metaphor, so that intention always remains somewhat open and somewhat elusive.[16] The purpose of such close reading is to go beyond our normal Western preoccupation, to go inside the text, and to engage the playful points of accent. Such an active engagement requires that the text is for hearing and not for silent reading.

The process of rhetorical analysis, in the simple process I propose, is not completed until a student reflects on what is seen through the analysis. In this case, the first two observations I make that arise from the analysis are these: (1) The subject of the prophecy moves from YHWH, God of Hosts, to the unnamed "nation." This poetic articulation of "double agency" (God and historical agent) makes clear that it is God's work that is done in the world in and through historical processes and historical actors.[17] Such double agency, accomplished so easily in the poetry, connects YHWH's purposeful governance to a concrete political-military force, a quite particular reference, but left open in the poetry for other particularities by remaining unnamed. (2) The prophecy is dominated by the four-fold "eat up" that may correspond to the four-fold *goy* and be further reinforced by the four word pairs of v. 17. The life of Judah, in all its treasured materiality, will be profoundly diminished until the life of the community is terminated.

Key Word Analysis

The second step I propose is to focus on words that are shown, through rhetorical analysis, to be crucial for the text. "Key word analysis" can be done by simple consultation with a concordance, preferably an "analyti-

16. The formula of Ricoeur, *The Symbolism of Evil*, 347–57, is an apt programmatic summary of the point: "The symbol gives rise to thought."

17. Articulation of YHWH's "acts" in the Old Testament are readily and easily linked to performance by human agents. I cite two obvious examples of this easy slide back and forth between human divine agencies. In Exod 3:7–9 YHWH asserts first person resolve to act on Israel's behalf. But in v. 10, it is Moses who is dispatched to perform the Exodus. This double agency is confirmed at the end of the narrative wherein Israel "believes in the Lord and in his servant Moses (Exod 14:31). In Judg 5:11 where the great victory is celebrated at the watering places:

> There they repeat the triumphs of YHWH,
> The triumphs of his peasantry in Israel.

This textual tradition perceived no problem in a double attribution.

cal" concordance that sorts out the Hebrew roots of words. But even if one does not work with Hebrew, one can learn a great deal from English usage. The purpose of such analysis is not to amass a statistical account of many uses, for that step is easy and not very productive. The important point is to check other uses of the term until one is able to identify other uses that are close enough to give nuance to our text, so that *other uses* may illuminate *this use*. Such a procedure requires great patience, as one must look through many texts before locating pertinent ones. The process is not simply to locate or site other uses, but sufficient to see that word usage performs the same function in their several contexts.

In our passage of Jeremiah, the obvious word with which to begin is "eat," "devour" (*'kl*). A quick scan of a concordance suggests that the four-fold usage of "eat" in our text is situated in a traditional practice whereby the verb speaks of historical destruction undertaken by an intrusive force, often understood as at the behest of YHWH. The usage is rooted in what may have been an old stylized formula of curse that comes upon a disobedient people:

> You shall perish among the nations, and the land of your enemies
> shall *devour* you. (Lev 26:38)

This curse reflects the tight calculus of covenant whereby disobedience yields covenant curses. The usage in our text indicates, then, that Jerusalem is under curse for disobedience that has been voiced in vv. 12–13 which will now be enacted, as in the old curse, by "your enemies."

From that covenantal tradition, a variety of texts make the same connection, linking the will of YHWH to the historical process, even though that will is hidden and not visible:

> Foreigners *devour* his strength,
>> but he does not know it;
> gray hairs are sprinkled upon him,
>> but he does not know it. (Hos 7:9)

>   *   *   *

> The sword rages in their cities,
>> it consumes their oracle-priests,
>> and *devours* because of their schemes. (Hos 11:6)

*   *   *

> Your country lies desolate,
>> your cities are burned with fire;
> in your very presence
>> aliens *devour* your land;
>> it is desolate, as overthrown by foreigners. (Isa 1:7)

The same usage is frequent in the Jeremiah tradition:

> Pour out your wrath on the nations that do not know you,
>> and on the peoples that do not call on your name;
> for they have *devoured* Jacob;
>> they have *devoured* him and consumed him,
>> and have laid waste his habitation. (Jer 10:25)

*   *   *

> Upon all the bare heights in the desert
>> spoilers have come;
> for the sword of YHWH *devours*
>> from one end of the land to the other;
>> no one shall be safe. (Jer 12:12)

*   *   *

> All who found them have *devoured* them, and their enemies have said, "We are not guilty, because they have sinned against YHWH, the true pasture, YHWH, the hope of their ancestors." (Jer 50:7)

*   *   *

> Israel is a hunted sheep driven away by lions. First the king of Assyria *devoured* it, and now at the end King Nebuchadrezzar of Babylon has gnawed its bones. (Jer 50:17)

*   *   *

King Nebuchadrezzar of Babylon has *devoured* me,

> he has crushed me;

he has made me an empty vessel,

> he has swallowed me like a monster;

he has filled his belly with my delicacies,

> he has spewed me out. (Jer 51:34)

Most remarkably, the same term in parallel usage can be reversed; now it is the enemies of Israel who are "eaten":

Then the Assyrian shall fall by a sword, not of mortals;

> and a sword, not of humans, shall *devour* him;

he shall flee from the sword,

> and his young men shall be put to forced labor. (Isa 31:8)

*   *   *

See, I am against you, says YHWH of hosts, and I will burn your chariots in smoke, and the sword shall *devour* your young lions; I will cut off your prey from the earth, and the voice of your messengers shall be heard no more. (Nah 2:13)

*   *   *

Look at your troops:

> they are women in your midst.

The gates of your land

> are wide open to your foes;

fire has *devoured* the bars of your gates. (Nah 3:13; see Jer 30:16)

The impact of the repeated usage in our passage is to make clear in emotive ways (a) the deep threat that the city faces, and (b) YHWH as the source of that threat that will be implicated by an unnamed military adversary.[18]

A second term evoking attention is "trust," (*bth*) , the capacity to find a source of staying power amid the vagaries of history. In its attempt

18. In the tradition of Jeremiah, Babylon, and more specifically Nebuchadnezzar, is regularly a double agent with YHWH in the treatment of Jerusalem. On Babylon in that tradition, see John Hill, *Friend or Foe? The Figure of Babylon in the Book of Jeremiah MT*.

to find its way around its geopolitical reality, Jerusalem sought alliances wherever it could find them; but the prophetic tradition characteristically viewed such alliances as acts of disobedience, because YHWH should be Jerusalem's only source of comfort and strength. The term occurs especially in the exchange with the taunting of Assyrians when Jerusalem is under threat:

> The Rabshakeh said to them, "Say to Hezekiah: Thus says the great king, the king of Assyria: On what do you base this confidence (*bṭḥ*) of yours? Do you think that mere words are strategy and power for war? On whom do you now rely (*bṭḥ*), that you have rebelled against me? See, you are relying (*bṭḥ*) on Egypt, that broken reed of a staff, which will pierce the hand of anyone who leans on it. Such is Pharaoh king of Egypt to all who rely (*bṭḥ*) on him. But if you say to me, 'We rely (*bṭḥ*) on YHWH our God,' is it not he whose high places and altars Hezekiah has removed, saying to Judah and to Jerusalem, 'You shall worship before this altar'? Come now, make a wager with my master the king of Assyria: I will give you two thousand horses, if you are able on your part to set riders on them. How then can you repulse a single captain among the least of my master's servants, when you rely on Egypt for chariots and for horsemen? Moreover, is it without YHWH that I have come up against this land to destroy it? YHWH said to me, Go up against this land, and destroy it." (Isa 36:4–10)

Other uses that reflect the same issue include the following:

> Do not put your *trust* in princes,
>> in mortals, in whom there is no help.
> When their breath departs, they return to the earth;
>> on that very day their plans perish. (Ps 146:3–4)

*   *   *

> Alas for those who go down to Egypt for help
>> and who rely on horses,
> who *trust* in chariots because they are many
>> and in horsemen because they are very strong,
> but do not look to the Holy One of Israel
>> or consult YHWH! (Isa 31:1)

* * *

What use is an idol

once its maker has shaped it—

a cast image, a teacher of lies?

For its maker *trusts* in what has been made,

though the product is only an idol that cannot speak! (Hab 2:18)

* * *

Thus says YHWH:

Cursed are those who *trust* in mere mortals

and make mere flesh their strength,

whose hearts turn away from YHWH. (Jer 17:5)

In our text trust in "the city" likely refers to armaments; but it may also indicate confidence in the temple and the icons that assure YHWH's guaranteeing presence in the city.

The four word-pairs in Jer 5:17, each of which has "eat up" as its verb, refers to the sum of Israel's material, historical well-being. These word pairs are used variously to suggest YHWH's blessing. Among the noteworthy uses is the enumeration of items that a king will tax:

> He said, "These will be the ways of the king who will reign over you: he will take your sons and appoint them to his chariots and to be his horsemen, and to run before his chariots; and he will appoint for himself commanders of thousands and commanders of fifties, and some to plow his ground and to reap his harvest, and to make his implements of war and the equipment of his chariots. He will take your daughters to be perfumers and cooks and bakers. He will take the best of your fields and vineyards and olive orchards and give them to his courtiers. He will take one-tenth of your grain and of your vineyards and give it to his officers and his courtiers. He will take your male and female slaves, and the best of your cattle and donkeys, and put them to his work. He will take one-tenth of your flocks, and you shall be his slaves." (1 Sam 8:11–17)

The list is not precisely the same, but here it includes harvest (v. 12), sons and daughters (vv. 11–13), vines (v. 14), and flocks (v. 17). In the vigorous statement of hope in Hab 3:17–18, the inventory concerns all that may be lost:

> Though the fig tree does not blossom,
>> and no fruit is on the vines;
> though the produce of the olive fails,
>> and the fields yield no food;
> though the flock is cut off from the fold,
>> and there is no herd in the stalls. (Hab 3:17)

Even given the variance, there is enough of a varying pattern to see the practice through which Israel's poetry regularly identified the several gifts of the creator that are placed in jeopardy when Israel violates covenant Torah.

These three forays into specific words help to intensify our sense of the judgment pronounced. The verbs and the four word pairs together communicate the loss that is to come in radical and concrete ways and the term "trust" roots the coming military disaster in theological reality.

The texts I have cited, to which others could readily be added, indicate the way in which our poem evokes in a thick way the sense of covenantal faith, and the cost of false trust whereby material blessings of every kind face jeopardy dispatched by YHWH. Jeremiah mobilized the sum of the poetic, covenantal tradition in his utterance in order to imagine how public life is construed when YHWH is at its center.

Social Analysis

Finally in my streamlined practice, I find it useful to ask of the text—in light of rhetorical analysis and key word analysis—"whose vested interest is voiced here?" This is not an easy question to ask, and not an obvious one as long as we are prone to ask "historical" questions. This third step is an attempt to move away from historical questions to focus upon the *contested social transactions* that are voiced or may be inferred from the text. Most of us who have studied Scripture are not attuned to this question and very many church people assume that the biblical text is neutral, objective, or innocent and therefore not enmeshed in contestation. This third point of study assumes that there are no neutral texts and that every text is, in some sense, an advocacy that enters into dispute with other advocacies that may be inferred or may be elsewhere voiced in the textual tradition. Behind this question lies a great deal of recent scholarship concerning the sociology of ancient Israel; that scholarship stretches from Norman Gottwald's study of the early period through Robert Wilson's sociological analysis of the prophets through Paul Hanson's identification of exilic/post-exilic trajectories to Morton Smith's identification of "parties" in the late period.[19] One does not need to know in detail all of this social analysis in order to be begin to ponder the disputatious character of the text and the parties to that contestation in any period of Israel's faith.[20]

A caveat: such a study of advocacy, dispute, and contestation has important implications for contemporary usage of the text in communities that take the text as Scripture. That is, we can engage the ancient dispute and thereby see the way some texts "work" in powerful ways in contemporary dispute. It is not the case—as some statements have mistakenly suggested—that this third step is an attempt to become contemporary with the text, to ask, "What does this text mean now?" That is not at all what I intend in this third step. It is to see that the text is a lively assertion in a community of listening and interpreting. Such serious interpretation happens only when matters are not settled and arguments must be made about perceptions and decisions now faced in the community.

The voice sounded in this text is that of an insistent public opinion operative in Jerusalem that is deeply critical of royal policy (and its social byproducts) and, consequently, is provisionally sympathetic to Babylonian policy that threatens Judah. Such sympathy makes it possible that an imperial policy may be seen as a vehicle for YHWH's sovereign intention.[21] That "public opinion" may be concretely situated in the family of Shaphan, a powerful political operator (see Jer 26:24; 36:10–12), and in the scribal family of Neriah (Jer 32:12; 36:4; 51:59), or critically in the circles of what became "the Deuteronomists." Such a social location identifies the poetic prophecy as one side of a deeply contested political dispute in Jerusalem.

19. Gottwald, *The Tribes of Yahweh*; Robert R. Wilson, *Prophecy and Society in Ancient Israel*; Paul D. Hanson, *The Dawn of Apocalyptic*; Morton Smith, *Palestinian Parties and Politics that Shaped the Old Testament*.

20. On the Old Testament as a contestation between competing testimonies, see Brueggemann, *Theology of the Old Testament*. While every such testimony is theologically serious, it is also the case that every such serious theological testimony is filtered through interest. It is the matter of competing interests that causes the text to be multi-voiced.

21. Thus in Jer 25:9 and 27:6 Nebuchadnezzar is referred to as "my servant."

This stream of influential public opinion may have been deeply pragmatic and concluded that it was futile to resist Babylon; beyond such pragmatism, this opinion was convinced that the policies of the Jerusalem monarchy were foolish and self-destructive. This interpretive trajectory, then, took steps to turn policy in Jerusalem away from such destructiveness by accepting the reality of Babylonian power that was construed as the work of YHWH. One may thus imagine (as in the prophetic advocacy of Hananiah in Jeremiah 28 and the anti-scroll activity of Jehoiachim in Jeremiah 36) that the royal house and its entourage deeply disputed the claim of the party represented by Jeremiah.

Given such a political opinion that views the destruction of Jerusalem as a result of self-indulgent socioeconomic policy, it is easy enough to see that in the canonizing process this expression of political opinion came to be accepted as a normative, theologically decisive judgment. The canonizing community accepted this political position as a theological verity matched by later texts in the tradition of Jeremiah itself, suggesting that the radical judgment against Jerusalem voiced here is penultimate. Ultimately—in the tradition of Jeremiah—it is the *goy* far away that is devoured according to the will of YHWH (see Jer 30:16).

To be sure, the Book of Jeremiah, in chapters 30–33 and 50–51, can look beyond the "devouring" of Jerusalem by Babylon. Such a long view assumes the caesura of destruction that became a decisive fact on the ground for Judah. Thus the poetic interpretation of being "eaten up" is actualized in the historical process, and so the poetic utterance is shown to be "true."

Hermeneutic

When this analysis is completed, it is not very difficult in the present-day U.S. to make a move to contemporaneity. It is clear that our society—harvest and food, sons and daughters, flocks and herds, vines and fig trees—are being "eaten up" by "a nation from far away." What remains in dispute and becomes the work of interpretation is whether that "nation from far away" is an outcome of divine dispatch. I do not believe that one can make a direct or simple move from text to contemporary interpretation. I do believe that such texts, taken seriously, fund an imagination with deep and pained awareness where we must struggle to see faithfully, as did these ancient poets. It is clear in any case that without such texts to ponder and to line out for us fresh dreams of public life, we will not have the resources with which to imagine the thickness of our life in God's world. Without such thickening texts, we are likely to settle for technical assessments and thin solutions that cover over the deep truth of our life in the world.

Four Characters, a Grudge, and the Place of God:
Genesis 50:15–21

THE ORIGINAL ESSAY ON THIS PASSAGE WAS WRITTEN AT A TIME WHEN
I was still trying to formulate and refine my own particular interpretive
procedures and methods. It was an attempt to move in an informed way
from historical-critical analysis toward theological exposition. It is evident in that paper that I was not yet very knowing or self-conscious about
my own interpretive procedures. Nonetheless the outline of how I would
proceed in more self-conscious ways is already evident in that paper. This
passage is rich and suggestive for interpretation; it features a narrative
voice that directs traffic, dialogue between the characters, and a theological perspective that evokes our interest.

Introduction

First I situated the text of Genesis in the midst of current historical-critical
work. At that time in Old Testament study, the text had been strongly read
by the two German giants in the field. On the one hand, Martin Noth, in
pursuit of large Pentateuchal themes, had seen the Joseph narrative as a
"bridge" that connected other larger themes.[1] On the other hand, Gerhard
von Rad was beginning his work on wisdom in ancient Israel that culminated in his last book, *Wisdom in Israel*.[2] Von Rad proposed in 1953 that
the Joseph story was a narrative portrayal of a model wisdom figure ready

---

1. Noth, *A History of Pentateuchal Traditions*, 208–13.
2. Von Rad, *Wisdom in Israel*.

for public leadership.[3] After Noth and von Rad, Old Testament scholarship, as noted in my article, was moving toward "canonical" interpretation, that is, to discover the editorial intentionality in the final form of the text, an enterprise practiced in various ways by Brevard S. Childs, David J. A. Clines, and Rolf Rendtorff.[4]

While my own work depends on those important scholarly contributions, it is evident that scholarship has been preoccupied with larger questions and, for the most part, has exhibited no specific interest in the smaller units of the text. The exception to that is von Rad, but even von Rad was primarily interested in expositing his sapiental hypothesis, and was interested in the specific texts only as they advanced that hypothesis. My own interest, in the context of this work, is to consider the interior complexity and intentionality of the text as it witnessed to the faith of Israel in its ongoing enterprise of transmission, revision, and interpretation. It is the *interior complexity and intentionality* of the text that continues to preoccupy me, for I believe that it is close reading of the artistic specificity of the text that has generative power. (I am glad to notice that such a focus has important parallels to the best practices of dynamic psychology and Object Relations theory, for focus there is also upon the intimate detail of specificity that has power to block or energy for newness.)

Rhetorical Analysis

In an inchoate way my paper practiced the methods that I have subsequently outlined with more precision. The first and most crucial step in that method is to present a rhetorical analysis of the text, treating the text as a complex system of interrelated signs, all of which are to be read as a coherent articulation of a "world" of interaction.[5] I proceeded in that article by the *identification of characters* and the *speeches* through which the characters interacted with each other.

The complexity of the plot features four characters, even though the principle transaction is between two characters, the "brothers" being pre-

3. Von Rad, "The Joseph Narrative and Ancient Wisdom."

4. Childs, *Introduction to the Old Testament as Scripture*; Clines, *The Theme of the Pentateuch*; and Rendtorff, *Canon and Theology*.

5. See Trible, *Rhetorical Criticism*.

sented in the narrative as a single character speaking with one voice and sharing one risk.

1. *The brothers* are the initiating characters who recognize their new situation of risk (v. 15). Their awareness of risk is evoked by the death of their father Jacob in the preceding paragraph (49:33—50:14). The brothers voice alarm because they face a new situation, given the death of Jacob,who had functioned to keep the family coherent and peaceable. The brothers have a prehistory of betrayal and abuse, having sold Joseph into slavery and placed his life at risk. Given that narrative plot, the brothers are alarmed for good reason. The brothers speak first in the exchange and pose an urgent petition to Joseph.

2. The counterpoint to the brothers is *Joseph*, to whom their petition is addressed. Unlike the brothers, Joseph's plotline has been one of inexplicable success, so that by the end of the narrative he is in a powerful, dominant position. At the end of our text, he will offer the decisive speech.

3. The third character is the father, *Jacob*. He is, of course, absent in this episode, having just died. But by his absence he is a decisive presence in the exchange, for it is his absence that creates the crisis that Joseph must negotiate with his brothers. It is impossible to overstate the importance of his absence for the narrative.

4. The fourth character is *God*, who participates in the scene only indirectly.

The brothers as well as Joseph allude to God as definitive presence. The brothers identify themselves as "servants of the God of your father" (v. 18). They do so in order to establish a positive claim for themselves; they affirm their faith as sons of Jacob. In the extended speech of Joseph that follows, God is mentioned twice. In v. 19 Joseph alludes to God in order to assert that it is God and not he who must forgive. This mention of God is designed to extend the tension of the narrative and to give Joseph breathing space in his response to his brothers. Joseph's second mention of God in v. 20 is more freighted, for Joseph "reports" God's intentionality. It is important that we have in the narrative no direct assertion from God, but only Joseph's "sovereign" declaration of a theological claim that is decisive for the narrative. Indeed because Joseph makes that preemptive theological declaration, we may observe that Joseph manages the plan of YHWH in the narrative and so gives indirect but unmistakable answer to his own question in v. 19. Yes, Joseph is in the place of God; yes, Joseph will respond to his brothers by making a God-freighted, God-like declaration. God is present here through the utterance of Joseph, no more than that, but no less than that.

Given this cast of characters, we may look more closely at the *exchange of speeches* in the text, for in Hebrew narrative it is speech (rather than action) that is characteristically decisive for the narrative. The speech of the brothers consists in three quite distinct elements. First, the brothers talk among themselves and pose the question that propels the narrative. They are anxious about their past history with Joseph (Gen 37:12–36), whether Joseph "bears a grudge" for past actions, and whether Joseph will retaliate in kind. They pose the question among themselves, but offer no answer. Instead they strategize about meeting Joseph. The second utterance of the brothers is an alleged quote from father Jacob; they mobilize the father to plead their case with Jacob's more powerful son. They seek forgiveness ("lift the transgression"), their transgression now being fully acknowledged. The brothers can offer no justification or excuse for their previous conduct, and so are fully dependent on Joseph's inclination. The third element of their speech is introduced in v. 17 with the dramatic and decisive particle, "now therefore" (*'attah*), a term whereby rhetoric regularly moves to a present tense petition. The petition of the brothers in this third element of speech reiterates the alleged petition of the father: "forgive." The three elements of the speech of the brothers follow sensibly and culminate with the urgent imperative petition. Everything now hangs in the balance and depends upon the response of brother Joseph.

Joseph will answer the petition of his brothers in vv. 19–21. The narrator, however, is not eager to rush to the resolution of the issue between the brothers. Consequently, before there is more speech, there is a narrative interlude that keeps the reader waiting, for we are offered no clue about Joseph's disposition (vv. 17b–18). In the interlude there is reported action: Joseph wept. We do not know and are not told the meaning of the weeping. It is surely reminiscent of his weeping when he first saw his brother Benjamin (Gen 43:30). But the weeping is open to a range of possible meanings and the narrator does not help us at all to understand. The brothers are also deeply moved and join in the weeping, following the lead of Joseph. We may imagine that this is, for the brothers without their

father, a profoundly liminal moment in which relationships are reconfig-
ured. The brothers do not know the outcome of such reconfiguring. And
so they dared speak one more time; indeed the freightedness of the moment requires them to speak. When they speak, they seek to redescribe
their relationship with Joseph in the most submissive, deferential terms:
"We are your slaves (v. 18). Joseph knows all about slaves who have no
rights and can offer no petition (Gen 47:25). The brothers recognize that
they are powerless and without claim, no longer brothers but now slaves.[6]
The brothers have seized the moment of weeping to make their ultimate
pitch to their powerful brother.

Finally Joseph speaks (vv. 19–21a). Only indirectly does Joseph acknowledge the petition of the brothers. He does not mention the forgiveness of his brothers, and he does not refer to their self-abasement before
him. But his initial response is alert to the petition for forgiveness, for he
asserts that only God can forgive. Thus he denies the petition. But before
that, Joseph utters a reassurance formula to his brothers: "Do not fear."
This utterance is characteristically only on the lips of God who has the
capacity to override fear by utterance.[7] Thus in effect Joseph does speak
"in the place of God." We should notice that there is a mismatch between
the petition of the brothers and the response of Joseph, for he does not
refer to the "crime" of the brothers that awaits forgiveness.

In fact, Joseph preempts that entire subject and moves on to a larger
issue, namely, the inscrutable working of God in and through the shabby
historical process of the family. Joseph makes a sweeping theological assertion in v. 20 that contrasts the intentionality of the brothers and the
more elemental intentionality of God. He claims that the suffering and
vicissitudes he has experienced at the behest of his brothers served God's
larger intentionality. The sentence turns on the transitional particle, "in
order," stating the purpose of God's hidden intentionality. That purpose is
to sustain a "numerous people," that is, the people of Abraham who are to
be as numerous as the sand of the seashore and the stars of the heavens.
The divine intention following the "in order to" thus links this narrative
to the larger horizon of the book of Genesis concerning Abraham's family

6. The strategic approach of the brothers to Joseph is not unlike the later son who
approaches the father in self-abasement in Luke 15:18–19. Whereas that self-abasing
approach is explicitly rejected in the parable, it is rejected indirectly in our text.

7. On the use of the reassurance formula in the Old Testament, see Miller, *They Cried
to the Lord*, 135–77.

and God's promise to that family. Thus the reassurance formula, "Do not fear," becomes the introduction of Israel to a new place, grounded now in God's providential purpose that is not deterred, even by the historical actions of the brothers.[8]

Joseph's speech concludes in v. 21 with a reiteration of the reassurance formula, "Do not fear," that is introduced by "and now" (*'attah*), the same transitional particle used by the brothers in v. 17. This second reassurance formula is of particular interest because it is followed by a characteristic formula of assurance that gives a reason not to fear, namely, Joseph will act decisively to sustain Israel (see 45:11). It is noteworthy that here it is Joseph, not God, who will maintain Israel, thus again placing Joseph "in the place of God."

After the responsive utterance of Joseph, the narrator adds a concluding formula of assurance (v. 21b). That formula is of special interest because the word rendered "reassured" is *nhm* and "speaking kindly" is a rendering of the phrase *'al-lev* that is literally "to the heart." This same combination of *nhm* and *'al-lev* occurs in the familiar text of Isa 40:1–2 in Isaiah's primal address of assurance to the exiles in Babylon, thus suggesting an utterance that decisively alters historical circumstance:

> Comfort, comfort (*nhm, nhm*) my people . . .
>
> Speak tenderly (*'al-lev*) to Jerusalem . . . (Isa 40:1–2)

The first element of my method is to offer a rhetorical analysis of the text from which a great deal can be discerned. The identification of four characters—brothers, Joseph, absent father Jacob, and God indirectly providential—provides the dramatic interaction of the text. The exchange of utterances yields a more-or-less symmetrical formulation:

Brothers' speech (vv. 15–17a):

- self-reflective question: "What if . . ."

- quote from father Jacob

- first appeal with *we'attah*

- petition

---

8. It is instructive that the same reassurance formula is pronounced at the start of the ancestral narrative in Gen 15:1. Unlike our text, there the assurance is in the mouth of God.

Narrative interlude that permits the brothers to voice their self-abasement (vv. 17b–18).

Joseph's speech of response (vv. 19–21a):

- reassurance formula

- preemptive question;

- theological verdict plus grounding in promise;

- reiterated reassurance formula introduced by "and now" (*we ʿattah*).

Narrative conclusion of assurance (v. 21b).

The speech pattern presents an incommensurate exchange between the brothers and Joseph, whereby Joseph (as usual) prevails; he sets the family on a new course of well-being by his preeminent authority. But his preemptive authority is in the service of God's providential commitment to Israel, voiced in the verdict of v. 20.

Key Word Analysis

My second methodological maneuver is to pay close attention to the words that surface through rhetorical analysis in order to see how the text mobilizes the characteristic uses of Israel in a particular way. Because I have already called some attention to such word usage, I need only list the important words here with slight notation.

- In the brothers' opening speech, we have noticed the combination of "grudge" (*śṭm*) and "payback" (*gml*) that together voice the anxiety of the brothers. The first of these terms occurs in Gen 27:41 with reference to Esau's resentment of Jacob, so that the fracture between brothers is reiterated in subsequent generations. The other term, *gml*, is a common word for "payback" that exposits the world of quid pro quo calculation in which the brothers live. The two terms together indicate why the brothers have such anxiety, because Joseph "owes" them a harsh payback.

- The reassurance formula, uttered twice by Joseph, is a formula that occurs in many places in Israel's rhetoric; it features a decisive intervention that causes a break in cycles of distress and anxiety.

As is often noticed, the formula is most often addressed to exiles with the articulation of divine utterance that breaks the dismay and despair of exile by a promise of a transformed circumstance affected by divine presence. In our usage, Joseph appears to take that divine capacity to himself.

- The double use of "intend" (*ḥšb*) functions to contrast the ill intent of the brothers toward Joseph and the alternative good purpose of YHWH that is known only to Joseph and here declared to his brothers in a life-altering utterance. The double use in Ps 33:10–11 that also contrasts the plans of conspiring peoples and the plans of YHWH. The same double use, in a context of exile, is offered in Isa 55:8, which contrasts YHWH's intent for Israelite homecoming and Israel's own despair about exile. In each case the "intent" of YHWH overrides the "facts on the ground."

Reference to these words indicates that our text is deeply situated in Israel's characteristic utterance, a pattern of articulation that provides for the overriding authority of YHWH and the result that Israel's (and here the brothers') perceived world is made to be penultimate, subject to the initiative of YHWH. Thus this cluster of terms that characterizes the interaction between the brothers and Joseph (and with the indirect participation of YHWH) means that through textual utterance reality is altered and redescribed. That is, the utterance of the text does not fit into or accommodate perceived reality, but effectively transforms it. The function of this text is to exhibit and effect the "strange new world of the Bible" that is out beyond the fearful world previously inhabited by the brothers (and by belated readers who identify with the brothers).

Social Analysis

My third methodological point is to consider the intention of the text in terms of social power. Within the text itself, it is clear that the defining social relationship is between Joseph and his kin, variously presented as "brothers," but also as "servants" to a master. That is, the self-abasing utterance of the brothers in v. 18 is crucial for the narrative. No doubt the abasement is strategic, in order to secure forgiveness from their powerful brother. But the statement also indicates a readiness to enter into a new relationship. Joseph, characteristically, does not respond to the self-abasement of the brothers, even to refute it. His ongoing comment signals that he refuses a master-slave relationship, even though he is preeminent and presumptive in his authority. The use of the terms Lord/servant" indicates an awareness of the power dynamics in the relationship. The brothers for good reason present themselves as "servants of Joseph." The reassurance verbalized by Joseph thus lives in tension with the assumptions of both the narrator and of the characters in the narrator. The force of his response is to insist that they are brothers who share a common destiny in the providence of God. In their anxiety, the brothers are prepared to submit. But such subservience is refused by Joseph through every part of his response. He is finally not "in the place of God." He is a brother who offers a good brotherly assurance by pushing beyond himself to the God of good and faithful intention.

If we move outside the text to ask about its function in its final form, we have many pointers to situate the text in the exile, not least the reassurance formula and the parallels to Isa 40:1–2 and 55:8. If we provisionally accept such a locus, then the assumed role of "servant" may reflect despairing submissiveness of the exiled Judeans to Babylon with a loss of covenantal identity; the identity of "brothers" insisted upon by Joseph through reference to the intention of YHWH is an affirmation that they are not servants in exile but heirs to a promise for a future which will be "provided" through God's promise enacted through human agency (Cyrus).

Conclusion

In canonical placement our text is located at the end of Genesis. It is placed at a moment in the text when the promise has run out. There is wonderment in the text (voiced by the brothers) whether there is any future for these brothers. As that wonderment is placed literarily at the end of Genesis, so that same wonderment is placed historically in the sixth-century exile of Judah in Babylon: Is there a way beyond this moment of hopeless "shutdown" wherein the brothers are prepared to become slaves (see Gen 47:19)? The text speaks powerfully in that situation and against resignation and despair.[9] The text asserts God's providential commitment

---

9. It is my judgment that "your thoughts," from which the poet calls Israel away, is

that is not contained in historical circumstance, but has its own future-creating force. Any future for Israel—for the brothers—depends on the fresh intervention of divine force. Thus the parallel between our text and Isa 55:6–9 (at the end of Second Isaiah according to common judgment!) suggests that in both cases (in the literature and in history) Israel's future—beyond the fear of the brothers and beyond the despair of the exiles—depends on YHWH's inscrutable providential purposes. Joseph is a spokesperson for such a defining possibility.

My comments here—that play from my earlier chapter—are designed to show how a concise, clear method can yield rich expository results. The sequence of (a) rhetorical analysis, (b) key word analysis, and (c) social analysis opens the way for what I take to be an important and compelling theological affirmation.

---

despair about a future from God. The summons then is to abandon a future of hopelessness for the sake of a new hope-filled future that God is about to enact.

CHAPTER 5

From Problem to Resolution in Four Scenes: First Samuel 1

Introduction

THERE IS NO ONE-SIZE-FITS-ALL COOKIE CUTTER WAY TO INTERPRET biblical texts. What one does with a particular text depends upon the nature of that particular text, its genre, its context, and its apparent intention. Nonetheless, there is something to learn about how to listen and how to see and what to watch for in a text. The effect of learning to read texts is cumulative. Every text to which we pay careful, competent attention adds to our capacity to pay more careful, more competent attention to the next text, even though the next text may be very different and may require a somewhat different approach. When I discussed Gen 50:15–21 in the preceding chapter, the text lent itself well to the general three-step approach in method that I had outlined previously, namely, rhetorical analysis, key word analysis, and social analysis.

The narrative text of First Samuel 1 pressed me in a somewhat different direction in a 1990 article.[1] As I scanned the text, two matters immediately struck me. First, the text vigorously moved from a *problem* (barrenness) to a *resolution* (new child), so that there is a dramatic coherence to the design of the narrative. Second, that dramatic coherence is accomplished through a series of clearly defined scenes in which each scene serves a particular purpose in the advance of the coherent whole.

---

1. Brueggemann, "I Samuel 1: A Sense of a Beginning."

I have learned from Phyllis Trible that with a narrative text the first thing to do in close reading is to divide the text into appropriate scenes, that is, to treat the text as though it were a screenplay that is designed for performance.[2] A scene is marked as a section of the text in which particular characters are presented in interaction with each other. To be sure, the biblical text does not explicitly offer stage directions such as "enter left" or "exit right." But in noticing scenes, the reader can easily discern who is present and participating in the narrative action and who is not, and therefore can imagine who has entered or exited the stage. When the scenes have been identified, then one can focus in detail on the *action* and/or the *speech* that occurs in a scene and, consequently, what has been accomplished in that dramatic moment toward the resolution of the whole.

Narrative Frame: Verses 1–2, 28b

As I took up the study of 1 Sam 1:1–28, I first identified the *frame* of the passage as *problem* and *resolution*. The problem of the narrative is stated in vv. 1–2. First the principle characters are introduced. Elkanah is given a detailed introduction in terms of his location and pedigree as an Ephraimite. The pedigree will be important when we come to his son Samuel, who is deeply grounded in Ephraimite tradition.[3] Mentioned with much less attention are his two wives, Peninnah and Hannah. The initial comment on them is terse. Peninnah had children, "Hannah had no children." The contrast is quick and sharp. We shall see that Peninnah plays no role in the narrative to follow, but is present as foil and contrast in order to intensify the crisis of Hannah. This framing would suggest that Elkanah will be the lead character in the narrative to follow. The narrative, however, holds a surprise; it will turn out that Hannah—scarcely mentioned in the introduction and without children—is the dominant character in what follows. This frame of the narrative presents for the reader a certain expectation, but that expectation is frustrated by the development of the narrative.

The conclusion of the narrative in v. 28b is terse and not without problem. There is a textual problem that must be acknowledged. (In my

2. Trible, *Rhetorical Criticism*.

3. On the Ephraimite tradition, see Wilson, *Prophecy and Society in Ancient Israel*, 135–51; more specifically on Samuel, see 169–84.

articulation of an interpretive method, I have not paid much attention to textual problems, because most people who study the text for the sake of the church [or for that matter in the academy] are not able to deal with textual problems with much competence, because textual problems constitute a highly technical matter. For the most part, one can at best compare available translations and make a choice, hopefully an informed choice.) The NRSV follows the Greek text in v. 28 and renders, "She [Hannah] left him [Samuel] there for the Lord." This concluding note gives closure to the narrative, declares that the problem of barrenness is fully overcome, and offers Hannah as a model of faith who keeps her costly vow to YHWH.

An alternative possibility is to consider the conclusion of the narrative in the Hebrew text that is offered as a footnote in NRSV: "He [Elkanah] worshiped there before the Lord." This conclusion draws attention back to Elkanah, who was accented in the initial framing of the narrative and away from Hannah; it also exhibits the entire family as pious and grateful to YHWH for the miracle of a son.

The interpreter may play with these two conclusions, and observe that the ongoing interpretive tradition was uncertain about a proper ending, whether to accent Elkanah or Hannah, whether to feature the father's piety or the mother's fidelity. The interpreter can, in any case, appreciate that there is more than one way to tell the story, as there is more than one way to tell every important story.[4] In acknowledging this openness in the process, the interpreter can introduce two important interpretive realities: (1) that the interpreter's presentation of the text is one rendering among many that are possible, and that the interpretation is a performance that could have been done differently, and (2) that this interpretation, like every interpretation, has a playful, artistic dimension to it. The text is not fixed and settled, but must be handled in a particular time and place for this performance, the purpose of which is to recruit the listener into the dramatic action of the text through the performance.

---

4. The capacity for more than one telling is evident, for example, in the way in which military winners tell the story, as over against those who have been defeated. The same is true in the storytelling of psychotherapy wherein the past can, in good faith, be reconstructed in more than one way. Indeed, courtroom testimony is yet another example of the same freedom in the exercise of constructive imagination.

Four Scenes

Once the framing of vv. 1–2, 28b is articulated, my reading begins to take up the several scenes in the drama. I have identified four scenes, though that decision itself is part of the performance that I purpose.

Scene One: Verses 3–8

The first scene features Elkanah, Hannah, and Peninnah. Peninnah appears only here, and her purpose is to "provoke her seriously" by the very fact that she, unlike Hannah, had children (vv. 3–8). The narrator is not interested in her, but focuses attention on Hannah who "wept and would not eat," shamed, angry, depressed about her barren status. Elkanah tries everything he can imagine to console her, caught as he is between his two wives who are deeply at odds with each other. He tries everything he can to assuage Hannah's state, including uncommon generosity. By the end of the scene, Elkanah is exasperated with his sad wife (v. 8). He asks her a series of questions that are partly inquiry, partly scolding, partly concern for her: "Why, why, why, am I not?" It is especially important that Hannah does not answer. She is too immobilized to respond. And so the reader must wait, as the scene ends as a powerful "downer."

One other observation on the first scene: YHWH is not an active player in the drama thus far. But YHWH is indirectly decisive for the scene. Twice it is asserted that YHWH "had closed her womb" (vv. 5, 6). There is no critical reflection in the narrative on this assertion. This articulation concerning Hannah is very different from the parallel statement concerning mother Sarah in the book of Genesis. There it is said only that, "Sarah was barren," but YHWH is not implicated (Gen 11:30). In the present case, by contrast, YHWH is centrally involved in the crisis that Hannah faces. As we will see, YHWH is a party to each scene in this drama.

Scene Two: Verses 9–18

In the second, more complex scene, Hannah continues to be the central character (vv. 9–18). The other active character in this scene is Eli, the priest at Shiloh. Noteworthy is the fact that Elkanah is completely absent in this scene. As the scene begins, Hannah weeps as she did in scene 1, only now her condition is intensified. She "was deeply distressed . . . and wept bitterly" (v. 10). But now she acts: She prays. She makes a vow:

> She made this vow: "O YHWH of hosts, if only you will look on
> the misery of your servant, and remember me, and not forget
> your servant, but will give to your servant a male child, then I will
> set him before you as a nazirite until the day of his death. He shall
> drink neither wine nor intoxicants, and no razor shall touch his
> head." (v. 11)

She promises to "YHWH of hosts" that a son given to her will be fully
devoted to YHWH; she will not keep the son for herself, much as she
wants a son.

Eli, the feeble priest, observes her silent prayer and misreads her action, judging that she is drunk. He rebukes her (v. 14). Now at last she
speaks out loud (v. 15). The narrator has kept her silent until now. She
voices her anxiety and vexation, but she does not tell Eli the specificity
of her trouble. The priest, like a good priest, does not need to know her
trouble. He blesses her and dismisses her in peace (v. 17). She expresses
her thanks to the priest and returns to her husband. She returns transformed. Now she eats and drinks (v. 18; contra v. 7). She is over her sad-
ness. Her truth-telling of vexation and need, plus a priestly assurance, has
decisively altered her life and her circumstance. The drama has begun its
move toward resolution.

Yet again YHWH figures decisively in the scene. Hannah addresses
YHWH silently with a vow (v. 11). Eli blesses her in the name of "the God
of Israel" (v. 17). That God is known to be a gift giver. The silent vow and
the uttered priestly blessing together permit YHWH to transform the life
of Hannah, and surely the life of Elkanah as well.

Scene Three: Verses 19–20

In the third brief scene, Elkanah reappears (vv. 19–20). The problem of
barrenness stated in the first scene is here resolved by a birth. Two features of this scene are noteworthy. First, YHWH is again present: "YHWH
remembered her." The line is terse. It does not indicate whether YHWH
remembered Hannah's forlornness in barrenness or Hannah's urgent vow
about the boy. We only know that YHWH, who is in the business of remembering those to whom YHWH is committed, here reaches toward
Hannah (v. 19). YHWH's remembering has performative force. A child is
born. The second feature is that Hannah speaks yet again. After she has
broken her depressed silence in scene 2 with a statement of her vexation,

the next speech comes to her more easily. Her world has turned by the attentiveness of YHWH. That divine attentiveness was evoked by her initial pain-filled utterance.

Scene Four: Verses 21–28a

The fourth scene is again longer and more complicated (vv. 21–28a). Elkanah is again present, though his participation is marginal, only enough to empower Hannah (v. 23). Hannah's primary counterpart in the scene is again Eli the priest. The scene concludes with the extended speech of Hannah who addresses Eli, recalls her vow, and acknowledges that YHWH has given the child in response to her petition (vv. 26–28a). Her speech culminates with yielding the boy to the purposes of YHWH.

Narrative Features

When I had finished tracing the four scenes, several matters had become obvious to me.

1. YHWH is present in or implicated in each scene. Indeed, the story cannot develop without the participation of YHWH—the one who closed her womb (vv. 5–6), who is evoked as blessing giver (v. 17), who remembered (v. 19), and who is acknowledged as giver (v. 27). Israel cannot imagine its world or tell its story without central reference to YHWH.

2. Hannah is the key character in every scene as barren, petitioner, mother, and giver. Her participation in each scene advances her speech as she moves from depressed silence in scene 1 through petition and naming to exuberant yielding in scene 4. While the poem of 2:1–10 lies beyond the narrative itself, that buoyant poem presents Hannah as one with full-throated, confident speech that is celebrative in every dimension. The narrative is a tracing of the way in which Hannah gains the power of speech.

   This is important for several reasons. Firstly, it makes the female character the primary actor. In a patriarchal society such as ancient Israel, placing the woman at the center of the story is remarkable. Secondly, she is not is not a passive pawn of the male characters but the one who initiates the action, makes the petition, bears the child, and presents the child. And thirdly, the story could presumably have been told from the vantage point of Elkanah, Penninah, or Eli.

3. Each scene is introduced by some verb of ascent: "used to go up" (ʿalah; v. 3), "arose" (qûm; v. 9), "rose early" (škm; v. 19), "went up" (ʿalah; v. 21). It should be noted concerning the complexity of scene 4 that in v. 24 there is another verb of ascent, "go up" (ʿalah). This is evidence of narrative freedom that does not always conform to our belated notions of symmetry. Likely too much should not be made of this sequence of introductory verbs; but without forcing too much on the sequence, these usages do seem to function as a series of stage diction. I would also suggest that by introducing each scene with these verbs of movement, the narrator highlights action and initiative, and the narrative is thus propelled forward.

4. Alongside YHWH and Hannah, each scene has a male participant who plays opposite Hannah. Elkanah figures importantly in scene 1, and is decisively present in scene 3. He is present in scene 4, but does not make any difference to the dramatic development of the scene. Eli, conversely, is present in scenes 2 and 4 but is absent in scenes 1 and 3. Thus it is possible to see that Elkanah and Eli alternate in their interaction with Hannah in scenes 1 and 3 and scenes 2 and 4 respectively, even though scene 4 is somewhat more complex.

The notice of these several features helps us to discern the narrative complexity of the whole and the dramatic achievement that is surely intentional for the storyteller.

Type-scenes

After I had identified the several *scenes* of the narrative and had paid attention to the growing *speech performance* of Hannah, it occurred to me to press further about the scenes through the notion of "type-scenes."[5] These are recurring patterns of human action and speech that are presented in familiar, conventional, highly stylized ways. Once the type-scene has been

5. The best presentation of type-scenes in the Old Testament is that of Robert Alter, *The Art of Biblical Narrative*, 47–62.

identified in its conventionality, then one can pay attention to the particularity and nuance that may be given to the convention in any particular usage. In contemporary film, one such "type-scene" is "the chase" that follows a familiar pattern but is each time given a twist of surprise. Currently the "chase scene" in *The Bourne Ultimatum* is an excellent example of the conventional type-scene.

In our present narrative, one may see that scenes 1 and 3 together constitute a type-scene of *barrenness* and *birth*. The barrenness of Hannah is given narrative specificity through her silence and inability to eat; obviously birth is an occasion for naming and for glad celebration. In general we may say that barrenness and birth evoke characteristic responses in every imaginable society, and the narrator makes use of that recurring human pattern. It is worth notice that these are the two scenes in the narrative in which Elkanah occupies a prominent place; after all, he is her husband!

It is obvious that scenes 2 and 4 articulate the statement of a *vow* and the *payment of a vow*, yet another conventional dramatic pattern. It is not a great surprise that the decisive male character in these scenes is Eli the priest, for vow and payment of vow characteristically entail a sacral action. Thus I observed through close rhetorical analysis that the narrative consists in the sequence of Elkanah and Eli scenes around the two themes of *barrenness–birth* and *vow–payment of vow*. These two conventional themes do not necessarily go together, but the narrator has shrewdly woven them into a coherent dramatic whole with sustained development that culminates in the relinquishment of the wondrously given child. It is no wonder that Hannah anticipates a "messiah" (anointed) who is to come to Israel at the behest of her child, Samuel (1 Sam 2:10). It is evident that the advancing power of Hannah's speech is indicative of the growing force of faith and confidence in Israel as it anticipates the gift of public power from YHWH. This may suggest that the subsequent reading of the narrative in later Israel is intended to be an act of empowerment by which belated generations in Israel moved, via the text, to confidence and power in the world.

Social Analysis

It is not necessary, after this close analysis, to pay too much more attention to individual words that occur in the text. I have already noted the "verbs of ascent" that seem to mark the scenes. Beyond that, attention might be given to the theme of barrenness, even though the term is not used in this narrative. It is commonplace, but worth noting, that in the ancestral narratives of Genesis, each of the "mothers in Israel" is barren (Gen 11:30; 25:21; 29:31). Specifically it is barren Rachel (Gen 29:31) whom YHWH "remembered" (Gen 30:22), an anticipation of our drama.

It is usual to notice the recurring use of *ša'al* ("ask") in our text (vv. 17, 20, 27–28). In addition to the affirmation that YHWH hears and responds, scholars have often suggested that the term alludes to *Saul* (*ša'ul*) who hovers at the edge of this narrative. That is a critical question worth asking, but it does not bear upon the narrative drama itself.

When we ask about social intentionality, we may imagine that the narrator had the problem, "How to begin the narrative of monarchy, especially after the concluding note of Judg 21:25.[6] Or conversely, the narrator might have asked, "How to begin a book of the Bible?"[7]

It is clear that the story of monarchy in Israel (and the story of 1 and 2 Samuel) is preoccupied with *David*, who first appears in the narrative in 1 Sam 16:1–13. But David must have had antecedents. The narrator went behind 16:1–13 from David back to *Saul* in 1 Samuel 9–11. But Saul must have had antecedents, so that the narrator works backward from Saul back to *Samuel* (1 Samuel 7–8), with a narrative recognition that Samuel is to be the definitive player in the formation of the monarchy:

> As Samuel grew up, YHWH was with him and let none of his words fall to the ground. And all Israel from Dan to Beersheba knew that Samuel was a trustworthy prophet of YHWH. YHWH continued to appear at Shiloh, for YHWH revealed himself to Samuel at Shiloh by the word of YHWH. And the word of Samuel came to all Israel. (1 Sam 3:19—4:1)[8]

6. This connection depends upon the recognition that in the Hebrew Bible the Books of Samuel follow immediately after the Book of Judges, the Book of Ruth being placed in a later part of the canon. In our familiar English Bibles, of course, a different ordering of book is followed that places Ruth between Judges and Samuel. Tod Linafeld has made vigorous case for the proper placement of Ruth between Judges and Samuel; *Ruth and Esther*, xvii–xxv.

7. The capacity to begin a book or story properly is a notoriously difficult and important matter. Perhaps the most famous "opening line" is that of Melville in *Moby Dick*, "Call me Ishmael." I titled my article on 1 Samuel, "A Sense of a Beginning" with intentional reference to Frank Kermode's important book on the Gospel of Mark, *The Sense of an Ending: Studies of the Theory of Fiction.*

8. It is clear that the narrators of 1 Samuel intend to portray Samuel as the kingmaker

Thus the narrative pivots on Samuel. But how to explain Samuel, his authority and his definitive vocation? Well, behind Samuel there is *Hannah*, his mother, who birthed him, named him, and devoted him to the purpose of YHWH, i.e., the experiment of Israel. But behind Hannah, there is nothing, no antecedent! The story begins in barrenness. There is no ground for anticipating that the story of Israel could come from such a beginning. This story begins in depression, silence, complaint, and petition, and eventually moves to exuberance. The story begins *ex nihilo*; Samuel is an inexplicable, miraculous *novum* that leaves Israel dazzled and grateful. Type-scenes have been arranged by the narrator in order to exhibit for Israel the wonder that Israel, as a public entity with identity and power, exists at all through the gift of YHWH. The gaining of voice by Hannah that I have traced through the narrative is a signal for the growing power of Israel, whereby this people that is small and insignificant in the world comes to well-being and fruition through the faithful remembering and the powerful generativity of YHWH.[9]

Conclusion

My study of this text has led me to three extrapolations that I believe are faithful to the intention of the text as it voices a trajectory of future possibility for Israel.

First, Patrick Miller has considered "the prayers of women in the Old Testament."[10] He suggests that Psalm 6 may be appropriately understood as a prayer of Hannah, or of someone like Hannah. The Psalm voices a complaint and petition that might have been on the lips of Hannah:

> Turn, O YHWH, save my life;
>
> > deliver me for the sake of your steadfast love.
>
> For in death there is no remembrance of you;
>
> > in Sheol who can give you praise?

in early Israel, with reference to both Saul and David. Saul's belated encounter with the dead Samuel in 1 Sam 28:3–29 indicates that Samuel continued to play a larger than life role in the imagination of Israel long after his demise.

9. The motif of "small and insignificant" continues to operate in David's prayer in 2 Sam 7:18–20, even as he is marked as the "eighth son" in his initial narrative in 1 Sam 16:11–13.

10. Miller, *They Cried to the Lord*, 233–43.

I am weary with my moaning;

> every night I flood my bed with tears;

> I drench my couch with my weeping.

My eyes waste away because of grief;

> they grow weak because of all my foes. (Ps 6:4–7)

Miller makes two telling observations about this characteristic prayer that pertain if we are able to imagine it in the context of Hannah's crisis. On the one hand, Hannah's problem of barrenness is YHWH's work:

> This oppressive situation is given only one cause in the Bible—God. Whether or not we believe this, the biblical story understands that the compassionate God of Israel has kept Hannah from bearing children.[11]

Such women must seek rescue from God, "who is part of the problem."[12] But on the other hand, the Psalm, characteristically, ends in thanksgiving, for the God who "closed" has "remembered:"

YHWH has heard my supplication;

> YHWH accepts my prayer.

All my enemies shall be ashamed and struck with terror;

> they shall turn back, and in a moment be put to shame. (Ps 6:9–10)

Miller's suggestion has the heuristic value of giving the Psalm the specificity of narrative in its voicing of need and thanks.

Second, there cannot be any doubt that the narrative of Hannah continued to be read and heard in Israel as an act of hope that could not be reiterated too many times. We may imagine that as the narrative was read and heard, Israel, in a variety of contexts of powerlessness, took on hope for possibilities that the world had judged impossible. In Isa 54:1–3, to cite an obvious case, Israel is portrayed as a barren woman to whom many children are given. While the text offers an explicit reference to Sarah, the barren mother of Israel, there is no doubt that the lingering narrative of Hannah would have thickened Israel's capacity for hope in this poetry.[13]

11. Ibid., 238–39.

12. Ibid., 239.

13. It is evident that the barrenness of Sarah continues to play in the imagination of Israel as appeal to her is made, through the citation of Isa 54:1 by Paul in his exposition

That same trajectory is surely taken up in Luke's portrayal of the births of John and Jesus, for they are gifts to women who had no reason to expect a child. Luke begins his narrative account of the gospel with an affirmation of impossibility (Luke 1:37), the kind of impossibility that recurringly generates futures for Israel. Miller concludes his study of the prayer of women:

> One thing further to note about this woman's prayer—and it is the transition also to a briefer attention to two other prayers of women—is that the concern about the things too marvelous or wonderful plays a part in women's stories elsewhere in the Scriptures . . . . When Mary bears the child and witnesses the human impossibility become possible with God, she sings a song of praise and thanksgiving that is derivative of an earlier song of thanksgiving prayed under similar circumstances, the song of Hannah. In these two songs of thanksgiving by two women of low estate, as humble and humbled as the one who prays in Psalm 131, we discover through their experience of God's marvelous deliverance what those things that are too wonderful for us but not for God: lifting up the lowly and putting down the mighty, feeding the hungry and giving sight to the blind, making the barren woman a joyous mother of children, God's power and intention to reverse those structures and realities of human existence that seem impossible to break. What we see in the prayers of thanksgiving of Hannah and Mary is that they have become, not investigators of the secrets of the universe, of God's order and power as manifest in nature and history (that is, the marvelous things), but *testifiers* to the impossibilities and wonders that cannot be figured out (Job 41:6; Prov 30:18; and Ecclesiastes) and were witnessed but all too often forgotten by "our fathers/ancestors" (Pss 78:11, 32; 106:7).[14]

Third, the process by which abused persons, most especially abused women, regain their lives has been much studied in the wake of the brutality of the twentieth century. In writing of abused persons in abused families, Judith Herman writes:

> Survivors who grew up in abusive families have often cooperated for years with a family rule of silence. In preserving the family

---

of grace in Galatians 3–4. The reference to Rachel in Matt 2:18 indicates that the entire matter of a barren mother was important for the reuse of these narratives. On Rachel as a continuing force in the narrative imagination of Israel, see Brueggemann, *Texts That Linger, Words that Explode*, 1–19.

14. Miller, *They Cried to the Lord*, 242–43.

secret, they carry the weight of a burden that does not belong to them. At this point in their recovery, survivors may choose to declare to their families that the rule of silence has been irrevocably broken. In so doing, they renounce the burden of shame, guilt, and responsibility, and place this burden on the perpetrator, where it properly belongs.[15]

The drama of speech amid silence is exactly the work of Hannah. She placed "this burden on the perpetrator," in this case YHWH. There is a widespread conviction that the practice of speech is crucial for recovery from abuse. In her exposition of the Rebekah narrative in Genesis, Elaine Scarry writes:

> they reassert not only the sensorially confirmable realness of their own existence (We are. We are. We are. We are.) but the sensorially confirmable realness of God's existence (He is. He is. He is. He is.), or in the voice that is attributed to him, "I am. I am. I am. I am."[16]

Scarry's intention in this statement seems to me profoundly complex. In any case her exposition contains a formulation of recovery through speech. The series of intense pronouns, "we . . . we . . . we . . . he . . . he . . . he . . . I . . . I . . . I," exhibit the intense interactive quality of (a) *self-assertion* in need, (b) address to the *perpetrator*, and (c) *solidarity* between "I" and "he" for the production of newness as a "we."

It is clear that the finding of voice and the assertion of one's existence and legitimacy is a recurring enterprise in ancient Israel, most particularly in the exilic and post-exilic periods under imperial aegis. It is equally clear that in the contemporary world, with seemingly limitless practices of abusiveness and brutality, that the generation of a *novum* through self-assertion to God is an urgent matter that can be grounded in this text. Hannah's self-assertion of need is kept grounded by her capacity to yield to YHWH as well as to petition. It is this dialogical practice of *demanding and yielding*, at the heart of this drama that is at the heart of every newness, ancient or contemporary.[17]

15. Herman, *Trauma and Recovery*, 200.

16. Elaine Scarry, *The Body in Pain*, 193.

17. On the cruciality of breaking the silence for the sake of the future, see Brueggemann, "Voice as Counter to Violence."

CHAPTER 6

Truthful Witnesses, Capacity for the Future,
and Responsibility: Isaiah 43, Habakkuk 3, Psalm 44

I INTEND—AND SEEK TO PRACTICE—A METHOD THAT CAN BE PRACTICED
with quick intentionality, that can be undertaken without excessive ex-
pertise and lingering over textual matters, and that opens the text to contemporary, faithful imagination. The purpose of such a practice is that
the text can guide to *redescription* and inform the *re-imagination* of the
world in which we are to practice faith. With reference to the text I have
considered from Jeremiah 5 in chapter 3, it takes only slight imagination
with the repeated word "devour" to connect to the "devouring" that now
occurs in the global-military economy. Almost anyone can enumerate the
"treasures" (sons–daughters, flocks–herds, vines–fig trees) that are at risk
in the contemporary world of a limitless U.S. power, insatiable modes of
terrorist threat, large concentrations of power and wealth to the exclusion
of many others, and the restless anxiety that stirs among both haves and
have-nots. Everyone can see that!

With that text from Jeremiah in view, everyone can entertain—for
at least a moment—that YHWH, the Lord of history, is in hidden ways
at work in the midst of the profound anxiety among us that cannot be
denied. I suspect that we take too much for granted the capacity to study
and ponder the Bible. How odd and how wondrous that in the midst of
contemporary *goi* who "eat up" social treasures, we are privileged to have
a poem of illumination, confrontation, and redemption that we take, in an
informed, critical naiveté, as God's own utterance to us. The text itself, in
its awesome durability, is cause enough for wonder.

It is a derivative wonder that teachers and pastors can lead many folks to engage the text. And these many folk, now as in long seasons of the past, find themselves addressed, re-described, and re-imagined by this "strange new world" in the Bible.[1] We have this capacity for illumination and confrontation given us in the text. More than that, we have this remarkable collage of many narratives, many prophecies, and many utterances from ancient folk who keep speaking with remarkable contemporaneity. In what follows, I will consider three other texts, yet again to articulate a simple, direct method of interpretation and to indicate the potential gains of such an exercise that can be replicated with many texts.

Isaiah 43:9–13

This poetic unit is set in the midst of Isaiah 40–55, a text commonly taken to be addressed to the deported Judeans in Babylon. The poet, in a swift move of imagination, creates an imagined courtroom in which Judeans and Babylonians meet to contest together over the true God.

Rhetorical Analysis

The rhetorical movement of the poetic unit begins with a *summons*, a *question*, and an *invitation* to testify:

> Let the nations gather,
>> let the peoples assemble;
> who declared this?
>> who foretold to us?
> Let them bring their witnesses;
>> let them hear and say, "It is true."

The pattern is a double reflexive verb ("let . . . let"), a double question, and then a double verb, "bring . . . proclaim." The effect is to put the Babylonians—the ones who are blind and deaf in v. 8—on notice that they must give an account of their truth claims. The verse culminates with "true" ('*emeth*) to be uttered by "witnesses" ('*edim*).

---

1. As noted elsewhere, the phrase is from Barth, "The Strange New World Within the Bible."

The poem turns abruptly in v. 10 with the strong independent pronoun, "You" (*'attah*) with the repeated term "witness." The double use of "witness" contrasts the alien witness in v. 9 and the Israelite witness of v. 10 who is "mine." The verse is direct address to Israel as "witness . . . chosen servant," and intends to authorize and empower Israel to speak the truth about YHWH, a reliable claim that contrasts with the false claims of Babylon. The intent is not that Israel should persuade Babylon, but that Israel should know and believe its own testimony concerning YHWH. The term "believe" is the same Hebrew term as "true" in v. 9, a reiteration that is crucial for the poem. Thus far the poem has *dismissed* false witnesses and *authorized* true witnesses. The term "witness" is used for both parties and both parties are subject to the issue of *truth*.

In v. 10c, the poem turns now to the first person assertion of YHWH, through which YHWH instructs his designated reliable witnesses about the testimony they are to offer in the court contest for truth. The divine self-assertion is a declaration of sovereignty and features a series of first person verbs:

> I am he;
>> I, I am the Lord;
>>> I declared;
>>>> I saved;
>>>>> I proclaimed;
>>>>>> I am God;
>>>>>>> I am he;
>>>>>>>> I work.

These self-assertions are matched by an almost incidental dismissal of opposing claims:

> no god was formed;
> no savior;
>> no strange god;
>>> no one who can deliver.

The assertion ends in v. 13 with a defiant rhetorical question: "Who can hinder?" The implied answer, of course, is "no one," certainly no other god. In the midst of this self-assertion, moreover, there is a reiteration from v. 10, "You are my witnesses." Thus the acknowledgment of *Israel as witness* and the substance of *Yahwistic testimony* are intertwined. Through this address by YHWH, Israel now knows who it is and what it is to say.

The sum of the parts amount to a three-fold field of pronouns: "they, you, I."

> *They*: Let the nations gather,
>
> > let the peoples assemble,
> >
> > > who declared this?
> > >
> > > who foretold to us?
> >
> > Let them bring their witnesses.
> >
> > Let them know and say, "It is *true*." (*'emeth*)

> *You*: You are my witnesses,
>
> > my servant whom I have chosen;
> >
> > You may know and *believe* and understand.

> *I*: I am he,
>
> > no God was found;
> >
> > I, I am the Lord,
> >
> > > no savior;
> >
> > I declared, saved, proclaimed,
> >
> > > no strange God.

> *You*: You are my witnesses,

> *I*: I am God;
>
> > I am he;
> >
> > > no one who can deliver;
> >
> > I work;
> >
> > who can hinder?

The rhetoric places Babylonian witnesses, Israelite witnesses, and YHWH in a triangle. The claim that "you are my witnesses," in v. 12, intrudes into divine self-announcement. That intrusion suggests that it is an accent point in the text. The future of YHWH and YHWH's witnesses cannot be separated from each other.[2] Everything concerning YHWH depends

---

2. On the linkage of YHWH and Israel as witness, Michael Oppenheim (*Speaking/ Writing of God*, 163) quotes a Midrash that he reiterates from a citation of Franz

upon Israel's readiness to assert and enact YHWH, even in the hostile environment of Babylon.

Thus the world evoked by the poetic unit is one of contestation in which YHWH—through Israel's testimony—will prevail even in the realm of the empire.

Key Word Analysis

There are in this poetic unit many primary candidates for key word analysis, not least the great verbs of rescue and transformation that YHWH claims for YHWH's self. I will focus on two words that are pertinent for the claim of the text. This text is all about the *witnesses* who in court offer rival testimonies about the truth of God. Not surprisingly the term is used for those who provide evidence to sustain a claim about power and legitimacy. I will refer to three uses of the term elsewhere that illuminate the usage in our text: (a) In Josh 24:22, Joshua negotiates with new recruits to the covenant of Israel, and warns them that the covenant requires rigorous obedience. He reminds them that their oath of allegiance to the covenant will stand against them as witnesses, and they agree: "We are witnesses." The encounter indicates that commitment to YHWH and to the community of YHWH depends upon truthful living that is congruent with YHWH. (b) In 1 Sam 12:5, Samuel, in his old age, seeks vindication of his leadership, and evokes YHWH as his guarantor and partisan against the critique of his contemporaries. Samuel asserts: "YHWH is my witness against you," and they agree, "He is witness." The term is used in a context of serious contestation, wherein the witness, in this case YHWH, is a truth-teller on behalf of Samuel's claim for vindication. (c) In a different kind of text in Job 16:19, Job appeals against his "friends," to a witness "in heaven" who will vindicate him. The usage is after Job's acknowledgment in v. 8 that his "shriveling" is witness against him, as though his disability verified his sin. Thus in v. 19 he appeals to a "better witness" to refute the testimony of his body.

All of these uses help us to understand that the term in our passage is about deep contestation. Israel is summoned to verify that YHWH is the true God and thereby to defeat the Babylonian testimony concern-

---

Rosenzweig:

> Isaiah 43:10: "You are my witnesses, says the Lord." The Rabbis interpreted this as meaning: "If you are my witnesses, I am God, but if you are not my witnesses, I am not God."

ing the fraudulent gods of the empire. In this usage, as in other texts, the "witness" is summoned in what amounts to a life or death issue about the fidelity of new covenant members (Josh 24:22), the vindication of Samuel (1 Sam 12:5), or the legitimacy of Job's claim for himself (Job 16:19).

The second term I review is the double use of *'amen* in vv. 9–10: "It is *true*... that you may know and *believe*." The noun *'emeth* (truth) is used to refer to reliable witnesses whose words correspond to reality. Thus in Prov 14:25 there is reference to a "truthful witness" who saves lives. Reliable testimony is indeed a life or death matter. In Ps 15:2, "speaking the truth," is a primal virtue among covenanters. The verb, used in Isa 43:10 ("believe") is used variously as "trust in YHWH." Thus in Exod 14:31 Israel receives evidence that YHWH (and Moses) is reliable. In Num 14:11 Israel complains and refuses to rely upon YHWH. And in Isa 7:9, King Ahaz is summoned by the prophet to trust. Thus the verbal form in Isa 43:10 concerns Israel's capacity to count on YHWH's liability, even in the midst of Babylonian power. The two uses in vv. 9–10 pose the urgent question, "On whom can Israel count?" The poetry makes a vigorous attestation for YHWH.

Advocacy

This *rhetorical analysis* and *key word analysis* prepare us to ask about a third matter: What is the *advocacy* of the text as a textual contestation? The issue between *opposing testimonies* raises the issue about whether Israelite faith claims have validity in the hostile environment of Babylon, or whether wise Judeans would do better to accept Babylonian definitions of reality and to sign on for that dominant imperial account of reality. Indeed, we may imagine that many displaced Judeans had, for reasons they thought obvious, signed on with the empire. This poetry is a rigorous summoning dissent that invites engagement in a world outside imperial hegemony. That new world which features YHWH as the defining character depends upon the truth-telling deportees. But that truth-telling depends in turn upon the utterance of the poet who authorizes such truth-telling testimony. It is clear, in such a venue, that such truth-telling is against the grain of visible power and, therefore, a high risk action.

This three-step procedure of *rhetorical analysis, key word analysis,* and *advocacy* yields an understanding of the text that continues to issue its summons. I have accepted the common (though not unchallenged) assumption of the exilic locus of the text. Given that, it is clear that the text can move into a contemporary challenged people of faith . . . whether to embrace *dominant construals of reality* or whether to trust *an alternative account of reality* that features YHWH and that refutes dominant claims. In that ancient world, as in the contemporary world, "God talk" about theological claims always brings with it an inescapable inference of political-economic power. "God talk" is never "innocent," but always has in purview concrete life or death decisions.[3] Thus the notion of "truthful testimony" requires a verdict.

Habakkuk 3:17–19

These verses that conclude the Book of Habakkuk come at the end of chapter 3, which exhibits a powerful disruptive theophany of the coming of God. While the theophanic characterization is likely older, in the context of Habakkuk at the end of the seventh century, the imagined upheaval may pertain to the soon-to-come destruction of Jerusalem. That characterization ends in 3:16, which refers to quivering lips, trembling steps, calamity, and attack. Given the negative force of that poetic imagery, we are astonished to read the counter-text of vv. 17–19 that offers a serene and confident assurance, the coming of calamity notwithstanding. In Hab 2:2, the prophet offers a vision of the future assured by God. These final verses urge reliance on that vision of a divinely guaranteed future. It is that vision, rather than the alarming facts on the ground, that matter for faithful living.

Rhetorical Analysis

This is one of those rare occasions when the rhetorical markers of the text are clearer in our usual English translations than in the Hebrew text itself. The translation of NRSV, for example, is a reliable one, but its rendering highlights the repeated cadences and the abrupt adversity more clearly than does the Hebrew. Verse 17 offers three parallel statements, each of which consists in two parts. The marker, in translation, is the three times reiterated "though" with six negatives in a variety of forms:

3. It was a great insight of Karl Marx, furthered by Michael Foucault, that truth always comes mediated to us through power. Marx understood from the outset that established truth is characteristically allied with dominant political and economic power.

> though . . . not blossom
>> . . . no fruit,
> though . . . fails,
>> . . . no food,
> though . . . cut off
>> . . . no herd.

The six parallel statements amount to a failure of creation and a shut-down of the food chain, a result of the resurgence of chaos portrayed in vv. 1–19.

The nouns that fill out these lines consist in three pairs, fig tree/vine, olive/field, flock/herd. (It is worth noting that two of these conventional word pairs—fig tree/vine, flock/herd—occur in Jer 5:17 as well, a text I discussed above.[4]) These two recurring word pairs—plus the other one here (olive field)—plus the other terms in Jer 5:17 (harvest/food, sons/daughters) in sum bespeak all of the blessings of an agricultural community and all of the measures of sustainable wealth. In this verse, as in Jer 5:17, the poetry affirms that all such material goods predictably will cease, the economy will fail, and social life will come to a halt. The three-fold "though" is not subjunctive. It is a conditional phrase, but affirms that this will surely come about.

The sharp adversative of v. 18 (translated as "yet," but given in the Hebrew only as a *waw*-consecutive), reverses field. The poet acknowledges all of the loss of v. 17; but then the poet refuses to be drawn into that failed world. The rhetorical refusal is made with reference to YHWH who is yet the guaranteeing God. Verse 18 containing three first person pronouns—"I, I, my"—is matched by three more in v. 19—"My, my, me." The speaking subject is reference to YHWH who is the ground of the refusal. "I will rejoice and exalt . . . because YHWH-God saves." That divine work of rescue is assured, even in the face of failed creation. Verse 19 is of another sort, but carries the same affirmation. Thus v. 18 leads with "I," but v. 19 accents YHWH as subject:

> *I* will rejoice . . . in YHWH;
>> *I* will exult . . . in the God of *my* salvation;
> *YHWH* is *my* strength;
>> *he* makes *my* feet.
>> *he* makes *me* tread.

4. See 40–52 above.

The verses feature both parties respectively, "I . . . YHWH," but v. 19 reverses the rhetoric to place the accent on the acting agency of YHWH. YHWH in fact is given only one verb (*sm*), but that verb governs both final phrases, and so the translation renders "makes . . . makes." The power of the rhetoric offers a dramatic contrast between v. 17 that details a *failed creation* and v. 19 that voices *the decisive agency of YHWH* who overrides the acknowledged facts on the ground.

Key Word Analysis

I have already indicated that the six nouns in Hab 3:17 constitute a conventional inventory of blessing and wealth. Again, as in Jer 5:17, reference may be made to the warning of 1 Sam 8:11–17. The same word of concrete reference to daily material life is offered in the blessing of Deut 28:3–6 and the curses of Deut 28:16–19. The reference to city/field, cattle/flock (vv. 3–4, 16–18) constitute an *inclusio* whereby everything is included from A to Z. The same inventory of material goods that are necessary to life is intended by the list in our v. 17. The same rhetorical intent of inclusiveness is at work in Ps 148:7–10:

> Praise the Lord from the earth,
>
>> you sea monsters and all deeps,
>
> fire and hail, snow and frost,
>
>> stormy wind fulfilling his command!
>
> Mountains and all hills,
>
>> fruit trees and all cedars!
>
> Wild animals and all cattle,
>
>> creeping things and flying birds!

The term "strength" in Hab 3:19 is of interest as a common term for wealth and for military strength. On *wealth* see Isa 60:5 and 61:6, which envision the wealth of the nations coming to Jerusalem. On *military strength*, see Exod 14:4, 9, 17, 28, which NRSV renders as "army." These are conventional and widespread uses. The term here suggests that in the face of the threat of chaos they will cause the cessation of creation; YHWH is Israel's wealth and military resources. Or as J. J. M. Roberts has it, "YHWH was Habakkuk's army."[5] YHWH as protector, guardian, and

---

5. Roberts, *Nahum, Habakkuk, and Zephaniah*, 158.

guarantor will assure a context of energy, freedom, and well-being. The usage of "fast feet," like those of a deer, anticipates Isa 40:31 wherein those who wait (hope) for YHWH,

> shall renew their strength,
>> they shall mount up with wings like eagles,
> they shall run and not be weary,
>> they shall walk and not faint. (Isa 40:31)

The term "wait" (hope) in Isa 40:31 is different from "wait" in Hab 2:3, but the point is the same. In both uses, such waiting consists in a refusal to give in to the data of failure, and to count on YHWH beyond failure.

Advocacy

It is clear that this text makes a powerful, specific urging to the community facing the failure of Jerusalem. There were in Jerusalem, perhaps, two prevailing moods. On the one hand there was, concerning the coming disaster, a sense articulated by Hananiah in Jeremiah 28, a refusal to be realistic about the coming calamity. On the other hand, there may well have been, as the calamity became clear and unavoidable, a sense of hopelessness that always lost. The twin temptations of *denial* and *despair* may have been very powerful in Jerusalem, denial rooted in Jerusalem theology, despair grounded in the awareness of Babylonian power.

Against both temptations the poet speaks. Against denial, v. 17 looks loss full in the face. It will happen! Verses 18–19, governed by the powerful adversity of "yet," refers to hope in the midst of coming loss; these verses counter the loss by appeal to Israel's ultimate resource and guarantor. The whole is an insistence when YHWH is confessed to be the primal actor in the life of the world, neither denial nor despair is appropriate. Either temptation makes perfectly compelling sense when "the world is without God." The poem insists, to the contrary, that the world is not "without God." YHWH is present as strength and savior. That alternative rendering of reality depends upon the poet.

Psalm 44:4–19, 23–26

My third text is Ps 44:4–19, 23–26. This Psalm is a complaint about some public crisis wherein the community of Israel has suffered and has been reduced to helpless shame. Verses 1–3 are a lyric affirmation of YHWH and I will begin with v. 4.

Rhetorical Analysis

This Psalm of complaint and petition moves through conventional steps of a communal complaint. Verses 4–8 are an acknowledgment that YHWH is the true ruler and source of life in Israel. It begins with the strong, independent pronoun, "You" (*ʾattah*) and celebrates YHWH:

> *You* . . . my king, my God . . .
>
> *You* . . . command
>
> through *You* . . .
>
> through *your* name.

Verse 6 is a disclosure about self-reliance, and v. 7 resumes the "You" statements:

> *You* saved . . .
>
> *You* put to confusion . . .
>
> thanks to *your* name.

These verses are a rhetorical setup for what follows. Verses 9–14 contains "You" statements. Except that they are now introduced by a powerful "yet" (*ʾaph*) of v. 9 that reverses the rhetoric. (This "yet" is not unlike the "yet" we have seen in Hab 3:18, except the reversal is now in the opposite direction.) Now comes a series of accusations, indicting YHWH for infidelity:

> Yet You have rejected,
>
> > You have abased,
> >
> > > You turned back,
> > >
> > > > You made us,
> > > >
> > > > > You scattered us,
> > > > >
> > > > > > You sold your people,
> > > > > >
> > > > > > > You made us,
> > > > > > >
> > > > > > > > You made us.

YHWH has acted as Israel's enemy. Verses 15–16 are a reflection on the outcome of YHWH's savage action:

disgrace,

>   shame,

>>   taunt,

>>>   revile,

>>>>   avenge.

Verses 17–18 assert the fidelity of Israel toward YHWH that contrasts with YHWH's infidelity:

>   we have not forgotten,

>>   we have not been false,

>>>   (we) have not turned back,

>>>>   (we) have not departed.

These two verses are, like vv. 4–8, a setup for another "yet" of accusation in v. 19:

>   Yet you have broken,

>>   you have covered.

The accusation and the statement of Israel's fidelity are summarized in v. 20–22. The "if" of v. 20 is a negative: we have not forgotten, we have not spread out our hands. God should know; but God does not know that, because we have not done it. The statement of innocence is followed by a third challenge, "because of you," following vv. 9 and 19.

This catalog of accusations and statements of innocence build to arrive at the urgent petition of vv. 23, 26:

>   rouse . . .

>>   awake . . .

>>>   rise . . .

>>>>   help . . .

>>>>>   redeem.

Even in these two sets of imperatives, there is more accusation and complaint against YHWH. The whole ends with an affirmation of appeal to YHWH's "steadfast love" which until now has failed Israel.

This is an extraordinary articulation in which the rhetorical moves are easy to follow. But for being easy to follow, they are—for that reason—no less astonishing. The claim is that *suffering* in Israel has not come from *disobedience*, but suffering has come from *divine fickleness*. (The argument is not unlike that of Job.) But the continuing alternation of *accusation* and *innocence* are only preparation. The accent is on the four-fold petition of vv. 23, 26. Remarkably, Israel must appeal precisely to the *God of faithfulness* whose faithfulness is here known to be reliable. The extended repetition of phrases in accusation and innocence is in order that *the sorry situation of Israel* and *the sorry failure of YHWH* should be given full and in-depth coverage. The purpose of such reiteration is to make the petition all the more demanding. For the community that listened to the entire poem, the imperatives must have come as a surprise. For YHWH who hears the prayer, the verses that precede the petition put YHWH in a posture wherein YHWH must, if YHWH cares at all, make a new saving initiative. The prayer, in its fullness, forces YHWH's hand.

Key Word Analysis

The rhetorical force of the Psalm is carried more by the reiterated pattern of speech than by any particular word. In this instance I would focus on the four petitions of vv. 23 and 26, even though the terms are familiar and widely used. The cluster of petitions to YHWH seeks to move YHWH to transformative action:

> *Rise up*, O Lord!
>> *Deliver* me, O my God!
> For you strike all my enemies on the cheek;
>> you break the teeth of the wicked. (Ps 3:7)

*   *   *

> *Rise up*, O Lord, in your anger;
>> lift yourself up against the fury of my enemies;
> *awake*, O my God;
>> you have appointed a judgment. (Ps 7:6)

*   *   *

> *Rouse* yourself, come to my help and see!
>
>> You, Lord God of hosts, are God of Israel.
>
> *Awake* to punish all the nations;
>
>> spare none of those who treacherously plot evil. (Ps 59:4b–5)

The same rhetoric is employed in Isa 51:9 that appeals to YHWH in a context of helpless displacement:

> *Awake, awake*, put on strength,
>
>> O arm of the Lord!
>
> *Awake*, as in days of old, ·
>
>> the generations of long ago! (Isa 51:9ab).[6]

The assumption in all of these usages is that YHWH has been variously absent, silent, neglectful, or indifferent. The urgency of the speech is to break the pattern of YHWH's neglect and to summon YHWH back into YHWH's characteristically faithful, transformative activity.[7] It is an indication of the dialogic force of Israel's faith to imagine that Israel, by its utterance, can evoke YHWH to new activity. But that clearly is the force and intent of this cluster of imperatives. The petition has such authority only by following the accusations and statements of innocence that have preceded. The hope of Israel is that YHWH will right the wrong of abuse that has been perpetrated against Israel.

Advocacy

The rhetorical force of "yet" and the petitions suggest a venue not only of trouble that is candidly described, but of disagreement about the cause of trouble and the remedy for trouble. One could imagine, given the calculus of "deeds–consequences" in Proverbs and in Deuteronomy and the dispute in the Book of Job, that there was a strong opinion in Israel that suffering is caused by Israel's disobedience.[8] If that is the cause of the trouble, then the remedy is Israel's repentance. Against such an opinion, this Psalm ad-

---

6. The same rhetoric is transposed in Isa 51:17 and 52:1 to urge Judah to action.

7. See Lindström, *Suffering and Sin*, 137.

8. On this theological trajectory, see Koch, "Is There a Doctrine of Retribution in the Old Testament?"; and Brueggemann, "The Shape of Old Testament Theology, I: Structure Legitimation."

vocates a different characterization of the crisis. It asserts that the cause of trouble is not Israelite disobedience but divine abuse. It follows, then, that the remedy is not Israelite repentance but divine re-engagement, hence the petition. What is contested is the extent to which YHWH can be called into question and held accountable, and the extent to which YHWH is beyond question and must be left out of contestation. The large issue the Psalm raises concerns the way in which covenantal existence is one in which both partners have voice and claim in conjuring the future.

Conclusion

The three texts I have considered, each in a distinct way, exhibit Israel's faith as a lively conversation of dispute and advocacy:[9]

- Isaiah 43:9–13 raises the issue about *truthful witnesses* that concerns YHWH's liveliness in public discourse.

- Habakkuk 3:17–19 insists upon facing the reality of loss, but nevertheless insists that *YHWH's capacity for the future* is unimpeded by the power of chaos.

- Psalm 44:4–26 insists upon Israelite innocence and *YHWH's responsibility* for the trouble that has come even in the face of Israel's faithfulness.

In each case a world is imagined with YHWH at its center. Without the text the world might be unmanageable and perpetually controlled by the empire (Isa 43:9–13), as a place of failed food production (Hab 3:17–19), and as a venue of public suffering for which Israel is accountable (Ps 44:4–26). In each case a deep theological claim is made; it is made in each case through daring and original speech. The only way to the *theological claim* is through patient attentiveness to the *rhetorical offer*.

---

9. See Brueggemann, *Theology of the Old Testament*, 117–44, 317–32.

CHAPTER 7

The Absence of God: Texts that Refuse to Be Explained Away

WHEN I CONCEIVED AND PREPARED THE ARTICLE ENTITLED, "TEXTS THAT Linger, Not Yet Overcome," I did so as part of a *Festschrift*—a volume of essays that celebrate a distinguished scholar—for James L. Crenshaw, a professional friend of mine with whom I have interacted in Old Testament studies since the beginning of our teaching careers.[1]

Crenshaw is a generative, prolific scholar whose many publications evidence high quality, scholarly craftsmanship. While his research is characteristically concerned with wisdom literature in the Old Testament, he is in fact consistently preoccupied with the most difficult interpretive questions concerning evil and the character of God in the midst of evil.[2] While Crenshaw gives his attention to ancient texts and ancient problems, he has in view the most acute contemporary issues of claims made for God in a world where evil is pervasive and palpable. As Crenshaw knows full well, these questions can never be fully and satisfactorily resolved. But it belongs both to the work of scholarship and to the struggle of faith to face these issues honestly, as Crenshaw has consistently done.

My intent in the article was to honor Crenshaw by taking up one small aspect of these questions about the ways in which God is presented in the Old Testament text. While these issues have been Crenshaw's peculiar domain in Old Testament study, I have also been engaged in these issues in a less direct way. This is evident in my articulation of what I have termed "counter testimony," by which I refer to Old Testament attestations

---

1. Brueggemann, "Texts that Linger, Not Yet Overcome."

2. For my positive appreciation of Crenshaw's "lingering" over these themes, see Brueggemann, "James. L. Crenshaw: Faith Lingering at the Edges."

about God that go against the grain of conventional, readily accepted biblical, theological categories that are acceptable and assumed in the church community.[3]

As is my wont, in this study I have sought to move outside the usual theological "explanations" for "the problem of God" in the Old Testament, for it seems clear to me that such "explanations" do not in fact "explain," and are often too easily reassuring or are voiced in rationalistic modes that disregard the quirky, irascible ways in which the Old Testament makes claims for God. My opening paragraph in the article seeks to acknowledge (a) connection to Crenshaw's work, (b) tension with theological convention, and (c) the focal problem of divine absence so clearly attested in some Old Testament texts.

> It is clear that God, as rendered in the Bible, is a continually unsettled character, and consequently an unending problem for theology, as theology has been conventionally done in the Christian West. The profound tension between the textual rendering of God and conventional theological settlements constitutes an ongoing interpretive problem for anyone who moves between text and a Christian interpretive community. No one has written more passionately or effectively on this issue than has James Crenshaw. . . . The problematic character of God in the text may be treated variously under the topics of wrath, anger, capriciousness, hiddenness, etc. Here I shall seek to advance the direction of Crenshaw's acute interest in the issue, in one small way by addressing the question of God's abandoning absence.[4]

In the preceding chapters in this present volume, I have reiterated (several times) my simplified method for reading texts, a method that I hope will serve those who must read while they run (Hab 2:2). Of that three-step procedure, here I have appealed especially to the second step, that of study of *major words* that carry the freight of the passage. The additional move I try to make in this paper is to move from the specificity of particular texts to a more generalized, thematic interpretive claim. This move is more difficult than we usually acknowledge, precisely because the intense particularity of biblical texts does not lend itself easily to generalization. As a consequence, our interpretive efforts tend to fail to make the move in one of two ways. On the one hand, we may just stay with

---

3. Brueggemann, *Theology of the Old Testament*, 317–403.

4. Brueggemann, "Texts that Linger," 21.

the particular without moving beyond the particular to a more general, thematic claim, a common enough practice for much Bible study and for textual preachers. But staying with only the particularity of one text does not go very far in making larger theological claims and, for the most part, readily misses the intense dynamism that arises when one text must have its say in the presence of other texts.

On the other hand, it is a common temptation to generalize without adequate support from specific texts. Conservatives are wont to say, "The Bible says . . . "; but that general claim is often not deeply based in texts, or a general claim is made on the basis of very few texts. Liberals, in a not very different fashion, like to say, "The biblical view is . . . ," again often without good textual basis or without taking into account all of the textual data. Thus when we make the move from *particular texts* to *general claim*, we may well recognize that the move is often not adequately based (because there are too many different texts) and often not adequately generalized (because the particular texts do not readily lend themselves to generalization).

Having said that, we must make the move of generalization in any case. We may do it with modesty, knowing that for almost every generalization we may make, there are texts to the contrary. In this discussion that focuses on divine absence, my procedure is a simple one. I have selected four texts to which I give some particular attention. Obviously many other texts might have been considered, and if considered would have yielded different interpretive outcomes. Thus the selection of texts from which we derive generalization is always somewhat arbitrary and subjective, and hardly ever disinterested. In this case, I have selected texts which utilize the verb 'azav with reference to God. By proceeding in this way it is evident that I have used "Step 2" of my simple approach—key word analysis—to locate the passages I will study. My hope in focusing on this word is to identify an interpretive space that Israel occupied as it dealt with the problematic way of God's presence in the midst of its life. Everything depends upon finding an adequate spread of texts for this exposition, and the appeal to this governing word, in this case, seemed a productive way to begin.

The term most often translated as "abandon" refers to the breaking of a relationship that was founded on fidelity so that the term is used for divorce, perhaps the quintessential transaction for departure from a relationship of fidelity. One notices at the outset that the term is quite concrete and refers to genuine face-to-face commitments over time. It is clear that the term refers to human interactions of fidelity and infidelity. Thus when the term is used with reference to YHWH—or to YHWH in relation to Israel by way of covenant—the text utilizes metaphors, playing with the likeness/unlikeness of divine habits of fidelity to human habits of fidelity.[5] In the use of these particular terms, we enter into the field of covenant, Israel's characteristic way of speaking about YHWH's mutual commitments with Israel (see Deut 26:17–19).

A great deal of scholarly attention has been given to the enormously complex matter of covenant. At the outset we may recognize that in Israel's usage, "covenant" stretches all the way from the *formal contractual* to *intimate emotional commitments.*[6] This wide range of nuances gives Israel's poets, singers, and narrators great latitude for the articulation of God. It gives them the space and resources required to articulate an interface between the character of God and the vicissitudes of Israel's historical existence, notably occasions of loss and displacement. In the end, I believe that generalizations about divine fickleness can be drawn, but such generalization depends upon the specificity of the text.

Before taking up specific texts, I call attention to the odd interface of this term "abandon" with the subject "YHWH." The phrase "YHWH abandons" gathers together succinctly all the acute trouble of Israel with YHWH. In Israel's founding narratives of the ancestors (in Genesis) and the exodus story, the accent is upon YHWH's faithful, transformative presence. Israel could not stay forever within its founding narratives. It had to move out of them into the reality of historical vexation, ambiguity, and threat. In that milieu, it found that the unambiguous claims for YHWH's presence no longer rang true. Therefore in its theological, covenantal rhetoric Israel had to voice theological vexation that is beyond the horizon of the founding narratives. One would not, at the outset, connect the subject YHWH with the verb "abandon." That connection is exactly what Israel's generative poets did, for they sought to speak the truth of life with YHWH in the midst of troubled history. It is that difficult interface that is our subject of discussion. In taking up that troubled interface, it is clear that these generative poets in Israel move in directions that are very odd from the perspective of the normative settled theological traditions

5. See Trible, *God and the Rhetoric of Sexuality*, 31–59 and passim.

6. See respectively William Moran, "The Ancient Near Eastern Background of the Love of God in Deuteronomy"; and more recently, Jacqueline E. Lapsley, "Feeling Our Way: Love for God in Deuteronomy."

of the church, for the church delights to claim that God is "omnipres-ent," always everywhere. Israel, characteristically, did not resonate with such sweeping universal claims. Rather, it focused on the particularity of a time, a place, and a circumstance. Given such a focus, there were times and places and circumstances in which it was not possible or credible to claim or imagine God present.[7] It is that concrete particularity that evokes from the poets of Israel the truth-telling that is considered in the interface of verb (*'azar*) and subject (YHWH). We will, given that problematic and that simple procedure of identifying texts by word usage, consider the texts in some detail.

Four Texts of Abandonment

Psalm 22

Perhaps the obvious place to begin is Ps 22:1:

> My God, my God, why have you *forsaken* me?
>
> Why are you so far from helping me,
>
> from the words of my groaning?

This characteristic complaint voices an accusation against God, suggesting that God's (seeming?) absence is unreasonable, unexpected, and inexcus-able and, in fact, reflects God's untrustworthiness. As is well known, this Psalm, with a series of "motivations" (vv. 3–5, 9–10), expresses a series of petitions that urge YHWH's presence and active intervention (vv. 11, 19–21a), and culminates in a celebration of rescue (vv. 21a–31). By the end of the poem this abandoning absence of God is overcome, and God is decisively present. We cannot permit the resolution at the end of the poem to nullify the experience and expression of absence at the begin-ning. No hint of fault, blame, or sin on the part of the speaker is expressed, as though the speaker's conduct justified the absence of God. It is clear that God is culpable in the intention of the speaker.

The accusation of v. 1, because it is a complaint, is in the mouth of the human (Israelite) speaker. Thus it is possible to say that the human voice has it wrong, that God is not absent but "seems" to be absent (on this, see below). For Christians this accusation against God takes on additional

---

7. On the struggle against the absence of God in the Psalms, see Lindström, *Suffering and Sin.*

gravity when it occurs on the lips of Jesus (Matt 27:46; Mark 15:34). It is a common theological strategy among Christians to explain away the abrasion of the opening lines of the psalm by observing that the line quoted in the Gospel narratives only introduces the whole implied psalm, again as though the implied ending nullifies the expressed beginning. In an important exception to this conventional Christian strategy, Jürgen Moltmann takes the gospel reiteration of Ps 22:1 with theological seriousness.[8] God is absent and is said to be absent. The narrative of the crucifixion of Jesus is a Christian articulation of that absence of God that causes the world to revert to chaos (Matt 27:51).

The juxtaposition of *complaint* and *trust* (expressed in vv. 1–2, 3–5) is characteristic of Psalms that voice the absence of YHWH. Israel lives in the double bind of adhesion to YHWH (having no alternative) and yet finds the Subject of trust to be absent from its life and without sustaining power for its life. It is not doubted that YHWH's presence will bring sustenance and transformation. For that reason, the work of complaint is to summon YHWH back into play, to evoke YHWH's active presence, for it is divine absence that permits the incursion of death and the reality of suffering:

> That the absence and presence of God are fundamental components in Ps 22's interpretation of suffering is apparent even by the way in which trust is expressed. The sufferer cries to his God YHWH (vv 20, 23). Evidently, this divine name alone has a sufficiently creative ability for the one plagued by the evil powers. The name of YHWH represents a previously won experience of God's presence, protection, and help against these diabolical forces (vv 9–11). Significantly, according to Ps 22:10, "it was you who took me from the womb; you made me confident on my mother's breast," trust in God is a gift given by YHWH. The basic attitude in man's relationship with God, that is, confidence, is inseparably united to the received, life-long experience of YHWH's saving presence.[9]

The "movement back and forth between complaint . . . and trust" is commensurate with *experienced divine absence* and *anticipated divine presence*.[10] Such a "back and forth" indicates the way in which Israel practiced

---

8. Moltmann, *The Crucified God*, 146–51, 207, 218.

9. Lindström, *Suffering and Sin*, 455.

10. Miller, *They Cried to the Lord*, 74.

dramatic theology, that is, theology as a dramatic performance in which characters come and go, enter and exit, and so are effective or irrelevant when off stage. The capacity to do theology as drama is definitional in ancient Israel, but for conventional church practice, such a theological interpretive capacity requires an immense unlearning of static, essentialist theological assumptions.[11] If one insists on such static theology, then one is likely required to conclude that divine absence is simply human misperception. The Psalmist had no such misperception, focused as the Psalm is on the concreteness of life. The Psalm could describe, vividly and in great detail, a social situation of threat in which one's very existence is at stake. Everything depends upon drawing YHWH back into the drama of life or death.

Lamentations 5

The capacity to explain Ps 22:1 away (because it is a human articulation of absence that may be a misperception of God) is an equally possible strategy in Lam 5:20:

> Why have you forgotten us completely?
>
> Why have you forsaken ('*azav*) us these many days?

Whereas Psalm 22 deals with an unspecified situation, Lam 5:20 is context specific. The verse pertains to the collapse of the symbolic (as well as political) world of Jerusalem (and of Judaism) over which Israel grieved massively. The physical loss experienced by Jews in the crisis of 587 B.C.E. is matched by the powerful sense of intimate, personal, religious loss. The destruction of Jerusalem signifies God's absence and happens as a consequence of God's (unwarranted?) absence. The interrogative form of 5:20 is the same as in Ps 22:1 with the interrogative conjunction *lamah* ("why"). The speaker does not question that God has abandoned. The abandonment by YHWH is taken as a given. In asking "why," the speaker does not seek an explanation from God, but seeks to assert that the absence of God is inexplicable and inexcusable.

Verse 20 is framed in the last strophe of vv. 19–22 by three striking assertions, each of which functions in relation to the desperate accusation of v. 20. In v. 19 the speaker utters a wondrous *doxology*, appealing to the

---

11. Most broadly on theology as drama, see von Balthasar, *Theo-drama*.

enthronement liturgies, acknowledging God's sovereign power. The effect
of this verse is to make the absence of v. 20 all the more scandalous, for
the one who "reigns forever" can hardly be absent. Verse 21 looks behind
v. 20 to v. 19, and on the basis of the doxology issues an urgent *imperative*
for God's action, thus characteristically following complaint with petition.
In spite of the doxology and petition the final verse (v. 22) returns to and
reasserts the *conclusion* of v. 20:

> But instead you have completely rejected us;
>
> you have been very angry with us.

And thus the poem ends. The accusatory verbs of v. 20 ("forget, abandon") are reinforced by "reject, be angry" (v. 22). Unlike Ps 22:1, there is
no resolution in this dread-filled complaint. The poem ends abruptly and
without any response from God. The effect is to confirm God's absence, a
fickle absence, and leaves the words "forget, abandon" ringing in Israel's
exilic ears.

These final verses of the Book of Lamentations give voice to Israel's
deep locus in the abyss of displacement. The poets of Israel eventually will
imagine Israel out of exile.[12] They will not do that easily or too soon. Nor
will they soften the critique of YHWH or let YHWH off the hook. They
aver that for whatever guilt Jerusalem may bear, the suffering of displaced
Israel is incommensurate with any identifiable guilt. And so YHWH, in
YHWH's absence, finally must be held accountable. And if YHWH's absence ("forget, forsake") is the root cause of dismay in Israel, then divine
presence re-given is the fundamental hope of exile. It is the fundamental
hope expressed in v. 21 with the imperatives, "restore, renew." But the accusation against YHWH in v. 20 prevails over any hopeful petition in v.
21. As a consequence, this poem of candor ends in v. 22 without hope. Tod
Linafelt deals with the difficult question of translation of v. 22, and finds
the "apodosis" that follows rejection deferred, but not cancelled:

> I want to propose here an alternative solution to the problem
> represented by this verse. It has often been noted that one might
> expect the phrase *kî 'im* to introduce a conditional statement,
> but that the second colon of 5:22 does not seem to state the con-
> sequence of the first as would be expected in a true conditional
> statement. While this is true, it does not rule out the condition-

---

12. On such imagining beyond displacement, see Brueggemann, *Hopeful Imagination*.

al nature of *kî ʾim*. Thus I have chosen to translate the line as a conditional statement that is left trailing off, leaving a protasis without an apodosis, or an "if" without a "then." The book is left opening out into the emptiness of God's nonresponse. By leaving a conditional statement dangling, the final verse leaves open the future of the ones lamenting. It is hardly a hopeful ending, for the missing but implied apodosis is surely negative, yet it does nevertheless defer that apodosis. And by arresting the movement from an "if" to a "then" the incomplete clause allows the reader, for a moment, to imagine the possibility of a different "then," and therefore a different future.[13]

For all the deferral, however, Linafelt notices the main point: YHWH does not answer!

> The appeal in 2:20–22, like the appeals made by Zion and the poet in chapters 1 and 2, remains unanswered. The voice of YHWH never sounds in the book of Lamentations; and as Westermann assures, before the move from lament to praise could be made, "first the most important thing had to occur: God's answer." Without such an answer, or perhaps some indication of a salvation oracle, the book of Lamentations remains incomplete. It evidences what Derrida has called a "structural unfinishedness." Nor is this incompletion easily imagined as one that is "carried to term," to return to the epigraph by Edmond Jabès with which I began this chapter. That is, it is not an incompletion that sits well with readers.[14]

Kathleen O'Connor, following the translation of Linafelt, draws the conclusion:

> The text expresses the community's doubt about God's care and about God's character. It utters the unthinkable—that God has utterly and permanently rejected them, cast them off in unrelenting anger. The verse is fearsome, a nightmare of abandonment, like a child's terror that the only ones who can protect her and give her a home have rejected her forever. Such is the ending of this book, and I think it is wonderful.
>
> It is wonderful because it is truthful, because it does not force hope prematurely, because it expresses what many in worlds of trauma and destruction know to be true. Its very unsettledness

13. Linafelt, *Surviving Lamentations*, 60–61.
14. Ibid., 61.

enables the book to be a house for sorrow, neither denied nor overcome with sentimental wishes, theological escapism, or premature closure. Although Lamentations does not tell the whole story and does not contain all there is to say about God's relationship to the world, it does tell truth about the human experience of suffering.[15]

Such a verdict does not "sit well." It does not sit well with conventional people of faith who offer the easy answer in "omnipresence." It does not sit well among the well off who cannot imagine such absence, and who regard such rhetoric as irresponsible regression. It dos not sit well in church practice that has screened out the hard texts and so cut off the hard part of life from theological discourse. But, as O'Connor sees, there are those with whom the text may "sit well," whose own life and memory know about divine absence reinforced by silence. In the powerful, unending, inundating wake of the *Shoah*, the beginning of the twentieth century is a tale of violence and abandonment. Unanswered Israel, and those who come after in this textual tradition, does not cease to "demand" answer:

> . . . the people close their prayer with a dispirited modification of their request: "Return us to yourself . . . unless you have utterly rejected us and are angry with us forever" (5:21–22). This verse has driven translators to their lexicons, concordances, and other ancient versions in search of a more positive translation. Hillers (100–101) and Linafelt (2001b) delineate numerous possible translations, ranging from turning the line into a question, "Or have you utterly rejected us?" (Westermann 1994, 210), to making God's rejection a past event over and done with, "Even though you greatly despised us and had been angry with us!" (Gordis 1974b, 151).
>
> But the book's final verse yields a happy ending only by distorting the Hebrew text. . . . But chapter 5 is not a penitential prayer—it is a demand that God see the people's pain and the conclusion is most appropriate.[16]

The act of "demand" is a measure of the depth of alienation and helplessness. It is also a sign of continued reliance upon YHWH in the midst of YHWH's abandonment. The poet can, on behalf of Israel, articulate

---

15. O'Connor, *Lamentations and the Tears of the World*, 79.
16. Ibid., 78–79.

what is most unbearable . . . God's silence. Israel, in its abyss, lives in an unvoiced present tense, and where unvoiced, without a future.

Isaiah 49

It is thought by many interpreters that Isaiah 40–55, in a quite intentional way, is a salvific response to the complaint from the abyss in the Book of Lamentations.[17] The abyss that remained "unanswered" in the Book of Lamentations now receives a full, eloquent answer of hope and assurance in the prophecy of Isaiah. Nowhere is that linkage more evident than in Isa 49:14–15 that seems to be a direct reference to, if not quote, from Lam 5:20. It appears that the poetry of 5:20 and its lyrical poetic context were taken up into repeated stylized liturgical usage. Thus Isa 49:14 begins, "But Zion said . . . ," quoting what Zion had said in its liturgies of complaint:

> But Zion said, "YHWH has forsaken me,
>
> > my Lord has forgotten me." (Isa 49:14)

To be sure, the two defining terms, ʿazav and sakah, are here in reverse order, but the intention is the same. The complaint, which we have already seen in Lam 5:20 as well as in Ps 22:1, is that YHWH is unfaithful and neglectful. It is YHWH's failure to be faithfully present in Israel that results in the suffering and shame of the exile.

The statement of v. 14 is lodged in the poetry of Isaiah in the midst of a proclamation of salvation, whereby the assurance of YHWH intends to dispute and overcome the accusatory claim of Israel. Thus in v. 13 YHWH is assigned two recurring words of assurance, "comfort" (nhm) and "compassion" (rhm). In direct response to the complaint of v. 14, YHWH now speaks in the first person, using the term "compassion" and three times "forget" by way of denying the accusation of v. 13. It is worth noting, though perhaps not important, that YHWH's response does not use a word to negate the accusation of ʿazav. The accent is placed on "forget" in the denial of YHWH.

Thus v. 14 as complaint and v. 15 as a divine oracle of answer constitute a clear example of Israel's characteristic practice of *complaint-petition* and *divine answer*. This clear connection between petition and answer, recurring in Israel, contrasts with the complaint of Lam 5:20 in which

---

17. See Linafelt, *Surviving Lamentations*, 62–79.

there is no answer. The divine response to lament in Isa 49:15 is quite remarkable:

> Can a woman forget her nursing child,
>
> > or show no compassion for the child of her womb?
>
> Even these may forget,
>
> > yet I will not forget you. (Isa 49:15)

In order to counter the accusation of "forget," the poet cites the primal imaginable case of bodily remembering, namely, that of mother and nursing child. The nursing mother will not forget the nursing child. The remembering of the mother is not only because of attachment and devotion, but is biological; if the child does not nurse, the breasts of the mother will eventually hurt. That hurt of the mother will cause the mother to remember the child.

Except that in this particular usage the text suggests that *even* such a nursing mother could conceivably forget the child. The most reliable rememberer can have forgotten! But not YHWH! YHWH remembers beyond a remembering mother. The imagery is daring. If we stay inside of the imagery, the remembering God is portrayed as a nursing mother whose breasts hurt from fullness.

The divine response offers a powerful play on words, as Phyllis Trible has demonstrated.[18] The term "womb" (*rhm*) in vv. 15 has the same consonants as "compassion" (*rhm*) in vv. 13, 15. The play upon the two terms produces a YHWH who is more compassionate than the compassion a mother has for her child. The divine response in v. 15 functions to overcome the cry of forsakenness in v. 14. Indeed a divine response of presence and attentiveness is required to defeat the experience of divine abandonment that wells up in the life of Israel.

Isaiah 54

Thus far all three texts (Ps 22:1; Lam 5:20; Isa 49:14) have been on the lips of Israel. This fact still allows for the claim that YHWH "seemed" to Israel to abandon, that Israel "experienced" abandonment, but in fact Israel had it wrong and was not abandoned by YHWH. Such a reading is possible, but it goes well beyond the plain sense of the text, which offers no quali-

18. See Trible, *God and the Rhetoric of Sexuality*, 50–51.

fication or ambiguity about the accusation. In these texts, Israel's claim of divine abandonment is taken at face value, without the characteristic hedges often proposed in the rationality of the church.

In our fourth text, Isa 54:7-8, that possible "protection" of YHWH from the accusation of Israel is excluded, for now the word *ʿazav* is on the lips of YHWH. The poetry uses the image of barren wife, abandoned wife, and widow. Already in v. 6 the term *ʿazav* is used in parallel to "cast off" (*maʾas*), both terms as passive participles, affirming that YHWH has taken the disruptive actions.

In vv. 7-8, YHWH continues to speak in the first person:

> For a brief moment I abandoned you (*ʿazavtîka*) . . .
>
> In overflowing wrath, for a moment
>
> I hid (*histartî*) my face from you . . .

The two words ("abandoned, hid") are straightforward and unambiguous. YHWH did abandon! YHWH has abandoned Israel and readily admits it. In these verses no blame is assigned to Israel as cause of the abandonment, though YHWH says, "In overflowing wrath." From the text itself, such "wrath" could as well be capriciousness on the part of YHWH as righteous, warranted indignation.

It is much the preference of church theology to make YHWH's judgment on Israel and YHWH's absence from Israel commensurate with and in response to Israel's disobedience. Patrick Miller has shown that divine judgment characteristically corresponds with precision to the affront of Israel.[19] In this text no such justification for divine abandonment is offered. The poetry leaves us with only the brute fact of divine abandonment. The divine voice that speaks an acknowledgment offers no explanation, and the poet does not seem interested in providing any possible explanation. This directness is enormously important, because it shows the way in which Israel resists any secondary theological explanation and chooses to deal with the concrete reality of its life.

To be sure, these two admissions whereby YHWH concedes that Israel has been abandoned are promptly countered by two assurances:

---

19. Miller, *Sin and Judgment in the Prophets.*

> . . . with great compassion (*raḥamîm*) I will gather you . . .
>
> . . . with everlasting love (*ḥesed ʿôlam*) I will have compassion on you (*raḥamtîka*).

It is profoundly important that the two positives do not nullify the two previous negatives. Here the statements refer to a sequence of actions and experiences, whereby compassion comes *after* an acknowledged abandonment. This is reinforced by the word "again" (*ʿôdh*) in v. 9 that admits one abandonment, but assures that there will not be a second one. This use of *ʿôdh* is closely paralleled to its use in Gen 8:21 and 9:11, which admits that there has indeed been one angry flood, but there will not be another (cf. Isa 54:10).

This fourth text, Isa 54:7–8, belongs in the same theological horizon as Ps 22:1; Lam 5:20; and Isa 49:14—all of which are preoccupied with Israel's experience of bereftment caused by YHWH's unwarranted inattentiveness. This fourth text is of another sort, because it is in YHWH's own mouth. YHWH concedes that compassion and everlasting love come *after* the abandonment.

Israel's reflection upon life with YHWH has this caesura of exile at its center. Israel can go for a long time in its pondering of reasons and explanations; in the end, however, it wants to move forward, not reflect backward. These four texts together—with their shared usage of the verb *ʿazav*—provide data for the acknowledgment that Israel's life in the world is marked by *divine abandonment* and *divine absence*. There is no way around it. YHWH does, from time to time, "exit" the drama of Israel's life.

Theology

In the tracing of my method, I have begun with a cluster of uses of the word "abandon" (*ʿazav*). The selection and justification for selection of texts for study is a crucial step in theological exposition. Thus far I have sought to read these four texts with reference to the term *ʿazav* that I have taken as a clue to and access point into a larger theological question. Having considered the four texts together, I seek now to take a step beyond exegesis toward theological generalization, a step that is risky at best. It is evident that we really do not have among us any clear method for that maneuver, which means that exegetes and theologians exercise great freedom in moving from *textual specificity* to *theological generalization*. In what follows I will consider the hard case of exegetical evidence for *divine abandonment* while church theology characteristically makes a claim for *divine omnipresence*.

We may identify five such strategies that are frequently employed in dealing with this difficult question.

Disregarded

It is easiest and most common to *disregard such "texts of darkness."* It is impossible to make use of all texts in any interpretive reading or all texts at once. It is surely impossible to attend to all of them if one wants to present a "seamless" reading, for the text itself is disjointed and disruptive; it is in many places filled with contradictions, ambiguities, and incongruities. Such features render the text as a whole "unreadable" in our usual theological efforts.

On the basis of that "unreadable" textual reality, reading communities of every kind, including church communities (but also academic communities), tend to be selective. Indeed, it is my judgment that serious readers tend to be "selective fundamentalists," whether liberal or conservative theological readers, or critical readers. That is, readers pick out texts on the basis of hidden or explicit criteria, take those texts with great attentiveness or even urgency, and let the other texts drop out of the working repertoire. An easy example of such selectivity is the church's lectionary, which operates around such close principles that even some verses in the chosen texts are habitually silenced. Part of recent hermeneutical activity is the insistence that those silenced, dismissed texts must be sounded again.

Justified

The "darkened" character of YHWH is justified by *the sin of Israel*, thus suggesting that God's silence, absence, wrath, or infidelity is warranted in light of Israel's sin and disobedience. Such an interpretive posture posits a tight moral structure, so that YHWH responds with precision to moral affront. There are many texts that support such a view.[20]

20. See the winsome discussion of Patrick D. Miller, "'Slow to Anger': The God of the Prophets."

There are other texts, including those we have cited, that do not claim such an exact calculus, or even suggest Israel's culpability. There are texts (as Job) that voice a "darkened" response of YHWH that is disproportionate to any available affront. There are sufficient texts to warrant the judgment that there is a "wild" dimension to YHWH's "darkness" that runs well beyond any tight moral equation. Israel's experience of YHWH's "darkness" runs well beyond moral justification when the texts are taken seriously.[21]

Misperceived

There is a great propensity to explain away the "darkened" aspect of YHWH (in our case abandonment) by claiming that the accusation made against YHWH and the desperate plea for presence addressed to God are a case of *human misperception and mistakenness*.[22] That is, God "seems" to be abandoning, but in truth is not. Such a human "experience" is asserted by Israel in good faith, and there may be a "subjective" dimension of reality to this claim, but it is theologically not true. It is only in the eyes of the beholder.

This suggestion of human misperception is not as difficult to claim in our first three cases (Ps 22:1; Lam 5:20; Isa 49:14), because the statements are all on the lips of Israel, and no data is offered beyond the "sense" of the speaker. Thus resort is often taken to the stratagem that claims that this is only "human speech," which is not finally reliable. The case is more difficult in Isa 54:7–8 where the utterance is YHWH's own, that is, a prophecy that purports to be God's utterance. Even here, of course, critical awareness can readily claim that even this speech is "human speech," done by a

21. On the violence of God and its immense practical implications, see Jeremy Young, *The Violence of God and the War on Terror*.

22. For powerful statement of this solution, see John Calvin (*Commentary on the Book of the Prophet Isaiah*, 140):

> When he says that he *forsook* his people, it is a sort of admission of the fact. We are adopted by God in such a manner that we cannot be rejected by him on account of the treachery of men; for he is faithful, so that he will not cast off or abandon his people. What the Prophet says in this passage must therefore refer to our feelings and to outward appearances, because we seem to be rejected by God when we do not perceive his presence and protection. And it is necessary that we should thus feel God's wrath... But we must also perceive his mercy; and because it is infinite and eternal, we shall find that all afflictions in comparison of it are light and momentary.

human author, in this case "Second Isaiah," so that even this more insistent affirmation is explained away as not theologically reliable.

This common interpretive procedure is deeply problematic. It appeals to theological-dogmatic convictions nowhere grounded in the particular texts, but imposed upon the text in order to dismiss a reading that, on the face of it, is not in doubt. If one explains away as "human and mistaken" such self-assertions made by YHWH, it is difficult to draw the line and treat the textual self-disclosures of YHWH with the seriousness that one prefers. It may be claimed that the dismissal of the assertion is "canonical," that is, read in relation to many other texts that say otherwise and are judged to be more central.[23] Such a claim is characteristically reductionist, and flattens the dialectic that, in my judgment, belongs properly to canonical reading.

Presence in Absence

A more subtle approach to this same "subjective" verdict voiced in the text is the logical, philosophical claim that even though YHWH is genuinely "experienced" as one who abandons, the experience of God's abandoning contains within it an assumption of cosmic, primordial presence, thus giving us a *dialectical notion of "presence in absence" or "absence in presence."* That is, even speculation about God's abandoning absence (which never posits God's non-existence) affirms God's "background" presence even in experienced absence. This is a quite sophisticated form of a "subjective-objective" distinction, which seeks to honor fully the *lived experience* of Israel, while at the same time guarding against an *ontological* dismissal of God that Israel would not countenance. This strategy is based upon the theological affirmation that there would be no world without God, no world in which to issue complaint and accusation against God, for the work is "held into existence" by God.

This is a powerful and logically coherent position, and I have no desire to combat it. I suggest only that (a) it is a way of reasoning that is subtle in ways that Israel would not entertain, and (b) it requires a judgment that is against the clear, uncomplicated, and unreserved statement

---

23. See Childs, *Biblical Theology of the Old and New Testaments*, reflects this conviction and practice. He also seems to suggest, in that volume, that the elusive notion of "canonical reading" is to read according to the "Rule of Faith."

of the text. As a result, even after this argument, we are still left with our guiding question, what shall one do with texts such as these.

Evolution

Finally, a popular stratagem is an appeal to the "evolution" of "the religion of Israel" that includes the "*evolution" of YHWH*, the subject of that religion. That hypothesis proposes that Israel's religion and Israel's God "developed" from primitivism to the nobility of "ethical monotheism," culminating, perhaps, in Second Isaiah. Thus, there may have been a time when Yahwism (and YHWH) were understood in quite primitive terms. There may have been a time when YHWH was excessively "dark" in terms of capriciousness, infidelity, violence, absence, and silence. But YHWH has "evolved" toward fidelity, peaceable generosity, justice, and forgiveness.

That hypothesis has long been duly critiqued as a reflection of Hegelianism or a reflection of a nineteenth-century milieu dominated by something like Darwinism. Nonetheless, there is something substantive to the hypothesis, as there regularly is in any hypothesis that captures scholarly imagination over a long period of time. It is the case that there are important changes in the character of YHWH. Given a certain literary analysis, one can insist upon a directional inclination to that change. It is the most standard critique of the hypothesis that the change is said to be progressive and unilaterally developmental. In addition to that claim, the critique that is most important for our purposes is the correlative of progressive developmentalism, that as each *novum* appears in the character of YHWH, the previous portrayals of the character of YHWH may be sloughed off as now irrelevant and "superseded."

$$\sim$$

I shall want to insist in what follows that textually, there is no supersessionism, but that what has transpired in the life of YHWH endures as texts, and therefore as data for theological understanding. This remembered character of YHWH continues to exercise important influence over the whole of Israel's articulation of YHWH. Specifically, because Israel has texts of God's abandoning, which it evidently has, the character of YHWH never completely outgrows or supersedes that remembered reality, which continues to be present textually and therefore substantively both for YHWH and the community of YHWH. As a consequence, neither YHWH nor the interpreters of YHWH may pretend that such behavior has not happened in the ongoing life of YHWH with Israel, and may not act as though these textual markings do not continue to be present and available to YHWH in YHWH's life with Israel.

When one credits the notion that YHWH's character "evolves," "develops," or "matures" through the long course of textual evidence, the "modern" way to handle such textual evidence is that the human makers of texts over time have become more sophisticated and less "primitive." That common judgment too easily credits changes in the divine character to changes in human understanding, and helps very little if one has a serious notion of Scripture as "revelatory." Given that usual view, the text can "reveal" nothing more than "human maturation," a judgment often made through the long history of modern interpretation.

If we approach the texts as a stratagem for "theological realism"—even in a "second naiveté"—then we may entertain the thought that YHWH, as a character in the life and imagination of Israel, is indeed a character who has a complex internal life and is indeed engaged in a process of maturation.[24] In taking this "realistic" slant on the text, I do not intend to make an appeal to what is commonly called "process theology," for that enterprise is much too abstract for what is faced in the biblical text. Nor do I mean to appeal to any form of "anthropomorphism," as though the sketch of the character of YHWH had not its own reference. I want, in a "naïve" way, to allow the text to have its own say without the embarrassments that come along with modernist thinking. It is on that basis that I have elsewhere suggested that the God of the Bible is indeed a "God in recovery" as a practitioner of violence, a violence that in one aspect consists in fickle abandonment.[25] And like anyone in "recovery," the recovery process for YHWH is always under way and never completed. I suggest that such a perspective on the texts of abandonment bring us close to the raw dimensions of faith in which Israel lived without flinching.

Thus I suggest that all five strategies—disregard of such texts, justification through sin, judgment that it only "seems so," philosophical subtlety, and evolutionary supersessionism—are unpersuasive approaches to the problem. Each of these attempts arises from a theological impetus that lies outside the horizon of the text itself, and each of them imports

24. On the theme, see Wallace, *The Second Naiveté*.
25. See Brueggemann, "The Recovering God of Hosea."

a conviction that is contrary to the unmistakable claim of the text itself. All of these inadequate strategies seek to protect the character of YHWH from the passionate experience and conviction of Israel with YHWH. Israel is clear that YHWH need not and cannot be protected; YHWH must run the risks that belong to YHWH's way of being present/absent in the memory and life of Israel.

An Alternative Response

I propose now to suggest an alternative interpretive response to these texts of abandonment and, by implication, to all texts that testify to YHWH's "darkened" life.

Drama

An alternative approach to these "darkened" texts will need to move from a *metaphysical* to a *dramatic* approach to interpretation. A conventional approach to Christian theology that posits a "nature of God" with which to challenge these texts apparently operates with a notion of a God "out there" that exists independent of these texts. Such a view may be plausible from some other perspective, but it is of little help in taking the specificity of the biblical text seriously. Such a posited "nature" outside the text stands as a criterion with which to justify or explain away a text without facing its concrete claim seriously. Indeed, such an approach cannot take such texts with theological seriousness, because matters are settled on grounds other than the text and in other arenas.

A consequence of such an approach is that we are still left with the problem of what to do with the text. An alternative approach that shuns the escape of a metaphysical criterion is to take the texts in a dramatic way, as a script for a drama. The biblical text then becomes "the real thing" in terms of plot and character, and there is no appeal behind the text or elsewhere. From such a perspective, when God asserts, "For a brief moment I have abandoned you," we have a God who abandons Israel for a brief moment. That is what YHWH says, what YHWH does, and who YHWH is.

The move toward a dramatic sense of the text permits the reading community to stay with the terms of the text, even with its contradictions, incongruities, and unwelcome lines. Thus the text is "unreadable," not because of a poor redactional outcome, but because the subject and character who dominates the plot does not conform to our flattened reading propensity, theological or critical. The character that once uttered these lines and committed these acts remains always the character that has once uttered these lines and committed these acts. There is more to this character than these particular utterances, but these lines become inescapably part of who this character is, no matter what other renderings, actions, and utterances may follow. That is, this approach comes to the text prepared to treat the text "realistically" and "literally," if "literal" means not "factual," not canonically reduced, but according to the concrete utterance of the text.

Rhetorical Man

But considering what it means to take the text "realistically," I have found enormously helpful the distinction of Richard Lanham between *homo seriosus* and *homo rhetoricus*. Lanham characterizes the model interpreter this way:

> The serious man possesses a central self, an irreducible identity. These selves combine into single, homogeneously real society which constitutes a referent reality . . . This referent society is in turn contained in a physical nature itself referential, standing "out there," independent of man.[26]

By contrast,

> Rhetorical man is an actor; his reality public, dramatic. His sense of identity, his self, depends on the reassurance of daily histrionic reenactment. He is thus centered in time and concrete local event. The lowest common denominator of his life is a social situation. And his motivations must be characteristically lucid, agonistic . . . He is thus committed to no single construction of the world; much rather, to prevailing in the game at hand.[27]

The important difference is that the "serious man" appeals to an "out there" reference. It is a curious fact that common cause in this category includes those who grasp at metaphysics and the "historical critics" who assess the rhetoric of the text in terms of an outside historical reference. Both metaphysicians and historical critics trim and shave the rhetoric of

26. Lanham, *The Motives of Eloquence*, 1.
27. Ibid., 4.

the text to fit some other criterion. By contrast, those who value rhetoric in a central way recognize that speech constitutes reality in some decisive way. The world of "Rhetorical Man" is

> teeming with roles, situations, strategies, interventions, but . . . no master role, no situation of situations, no strategy for outflanking all strategies . . . no neutral point of rationality from the vantage point of which the 'merely rhetorical' can be identified and held in check.[28]

It is clear that this dispute is as old as Plato and Aristotle with the Sophists. And it is clear that our dominant educational, intellectual tradition is a powerful advocacy toward Plato and Aristotle and a facile dismissal of the Sophists, without attending to the powerful ways in which even Plato and Aristotle are rhetoricians. See the distinction pressed further and clarified by Richard Rorty.[29] It suggests that even the "serious man" in fact makes a claim for reality in terms of the effectiveness of utterance.

What to do with the "dark texts" depends upon where one is in this dispute between rhetoric and "seriousness." If one "seriously" assumes a reference out there, then these texts must be disregarded, toned down, justified, or explained away, in order to suit that outside reference. If we take *rhetoric as constitutive* then the reference "inside the drama" must yield to these texts and take them with defining seriousness. Focus on the text rather than on a reference "out there" gives us no character other than this one.

Childs and Blumenthal

We are not yet agreed on what it means to take the text seriously or how to take the text seriously. I cite two interpreters who well articulate what I regard as two quite distinct alternative approaches.

In his "canonical approach" to the text, Brevard Childs is a "serious" reader who does indeed take the text seriously. That is beyond question. In a series of books, Childs has pondered "canonical" reading. In his most recent and most mature book, it is now clearer than in his earlier works that Childs means by "canonical" reading the text according to Christian doctrinal norms and categories:

28. Fish, "Rhetoric," 215.

29. Rorty, *Consequences of Pragmatism*, 92; quoted in ibid., 221.

It is one thing to suggest that biblical scholars have not adequately resolved the problem of biblical referentiality; it is quite another to suggest that it is a non-issue. Moreover, I would argue that the attempt of many literary critics to by-pass the problem of biblical reality and refuse to distinguish between text and the reality of its subject matter severely cripples the theological enterprise of Biblical Theology. It is basic to Christian theology to reckon with an extra-biblical reality, namely with the resurrected Christ who evoked the New Testament Witness. When H. Frei, in one of his last essays, spoke of 'midrash' as a text-creating reality, he moved in a direction, in my opinion, which for Christian theology can only end in failure.[30]

In his response to Stanley Hauerwas and James Barr, Childs concludes that "narrative interpretation"

> avoids for a time the difficult problems of referentiality involved in the term history . . . In a word, the term "story" is not strong enough to support the function assigned to the Bible. Indeed Christians have always believed that we are not saved by a text or by a narrative, but by the life, death, and resurrection of Jesus Christ in time and space.[31]

It becomes clear that Childs's understanding of God in the text, an "extra-biblical reality," is not construed or nuanced according to the detail of the text, but is a reference that is known apart from and at times over against the text. This theological reference must move "from a description of the biblical witnesses to the object toward which these witnesses point, that is, to their subject matter, substance, or *res*."[32] Childs's comments following this statement indicate that he is aware of the dangers in what he suggests, but he proceeds on that basis. Childs is interested in "the reality constitutive of these biblical witnesses." That "reality" is not only "testified to in the Bible." It is "that living reality known and experienced as the exalted Christ through the Holy Spirit within the present community of faith."[33] In such an christological formulation as Childs makes central to his perspective, the text as such is subordinated to other claims. A conse-

30. Childs, *Biblical Theology of the Old Testament and New Testaments*, 20.

31. Ibid., 665.

32. Ibid, 80.

33. Ibid, 86.

quence is that the "dark texts" exercise almost no influence upon Childs's interpretation and argument.

A sharp contrast to the approach of Childs occurs in the powerful work of David Blumenthal, who takes his beginning points from the brutality of the holocaust. In contrast to the "canonical reading" of Childs, Blumenthal reads texts *"seriatim . . .* one after another, one by one in succession, which matches the way we live. "We live *seriatim*."[34] This approach yields an accent upon "caesura, fragmentedness, irruption," the very matters that Childs wants to exclude.

With relentless determination, Blumenthal insists upon attending to all the texts:

> By contrast, I choose to engage seriously the texts as we have received them . . . There is, thus, for me, a certain sacredness to the tradition, prima facie, and I try to work within it. For this reason, I reject attempts to "clean up" the Psalms, to interpret away the rage, to make them more "pious."[35]

Blumenthal mentions, as we have also, that historicism and an assumption of moral evolution are two ways to dispose of parts of the text with which one does not agree. Not surprisingly, he rejects any such maneuver. By attending *seriatim* to all of the texts, Blumenthal comes to the interpretive conclusion that the God of the Bible "is abusive, but not always." In any case, he makes much room for "dark" texts that Childs drops from purview.

It is important that both Blumenthal and Childs allow for plurivocity in the text. Blumenthal judges,

> In the end, the text has more than one meaning, the reader reads on more than one level, and the teacher teaches more than one meaning. Text and life itself are multifaceted; interpretation is multidimensional. Plurivocity is normal; not hierarchy, not the single authoritative teaching . . . Plurivocity is, thus, not only normal; it is normative, it is what the norm should be.[36]

Childs agrees, "There is a 'reader response' required by any responsible theological reflection." But Childs qualifies such an allowance:

34. Blumenthal, *Facing the Abusing God*, 48.
35. Ibid, 238.
36. Ibid, 239.

> Yet it is crucial to theological reflection that canonical restraints
> be used and that reader response be critically tested in the light
> of different witnesses of the whole Bible . . . There is a biblical
> rule of faith which sets the standard for family resemblance . . .
> Once the task of discerning the kerygmatic content of the wit-
> nesses has been pursued, it is fully in order to offer an analogi-
> cal extension of this kerygmatic message by means of a modern
> reader response.[37]

This qualification causes Childs to part decisively from Blumenthal in the
end, concerning "dark" texts.

The difference between Childs and Blumenthal turns on *which texts*
and *how to read the texts*. It may be that the ground of the differences
lie in the difference of a Christian and a Jew, a Christian more inclined
toward *systematization* that requires texts to fit a larger frame, a Jew who
will proceed *ad seriatim*. These different approaches do not need to be
assigned respectively to Jew and Christian, for Christians also may pay
more attention to texts without imposing on them a reductionist master
narrative.

Naïve Realism

That still leaves us with the question of what to do with these texts that are
there, as Blumenthal insists, but texts that are enormously problematic, as
Childs insists. My suggestion is that we take a "naïvely realistic" view of the
text as a "script" of YHWH's past.[38] Such naïveté, for this purpose, overrides our critical judgments. Without a hypothesis of moral evolution, it
is clear that YHWH "moves on" as a character in the text, as any character
surely will move on in the drama. Thus these texts are in YHWH's *past*,
but they are assuredly *in* YHWH's past. I propose, with an analogue from
"the enduring power of the past" in therapeutic categories, that the "past
texts" are enduringly painful memories still available to the character of
YHWH, mostly not operative, but continuing to work even in the present.[39] They must therefore be taken seriously even in the canonical "final
form" of the text.

37. Childs, *Biblical Theology of the Old and New Testaments*, 335–36.

38. Note Jack Miles's sequential reading in *God: A Biography*.

39. This crucial matter in ancient Israel anticipates the aphorism of William Faulkner
that the past is "not even past."

This means that a "truer" picture of YHWH cast in canonical or theological form has moved beyond these texts, but has not superseded these texts, as no human person understood in depth ever supersedes or scuttles or outgrows such ancient and powerful memories. There linger in the character of YHWH ancient memories (texts) that belong to the "density" of YHWH and that form a crucial residue of YHWH's character. YHWH may not be in a "truer" "canonical" understanding, a God who abandons. But that past marking of YHWH is still potentially available in the current life of YHWH (for the text lingers), and must in any case be taken as a crucial part of the career of YHWH. YHWH cannot simply will away that past, nor can the interpreters of YHWH.

For the interpreting community (especially for the religious communities of interpretation, but also for the academic community) that intends to face the fullness of the text, the witness to YHWH and the interpreters of the witness must take into serious account that past and those memories that are in important ways still present, available, and potentially operative. This in turn suggests that it is faithful to the text and healthy for the reading community that there is, in this textual memory, an unsettling dimension that has wounded, troubled, and betrayed those with whom YHWH interacts. This past of wound, trouble, and betrayal, moreover, still tells in the present. I suggest that such a recovery of the past is not like "critical excavation," for it is not a past that is over and done, but a past that persists like any such held script. Full embrace of such texts permits the interpretive community to embrace fully its theological past, which is marked by abandonment (and other dimensions of "darkness"). It is not necessary to claim that such a "dark" dimension is normative or presently operative, but only that it has been there in the past and continues to be present in our reading. Thus the God of "steadfast love and mercy" is also the God who has abandoned, and all current steadfastness bears the wounding mark of that ancient, undenied reality.

Such an interpretive strategy affirms that the canonical text is indeed the full telling of the tale of YHWH, a tale that has odd and unpleasant dimensions to it.

As an interpretive perspective, such a procedure permits some thematic closure in the direction that Childs wants to go, but not such a closure that it eliminates the candor of the text itself, which has generated the candor of Blumenthal. It occurs to me that while many historical critics insistently resist Childs's closure, such historical critics finally make common cause with Childs, though for very different reasons. Childs tends to shave the text to fit "the creed," whereas historical critics have tended to shave the text to fit Enlightenment reasonableness that wants to eliminate disruption and incongruity in the text. Neither "canonical" nor "critical" readers entertain the naïveté to permit a rendering of the text as the dramatic reality of this God with this people.

But my primary concern is not interpretive theory. My concern is pastoral responsibility, the kind of pastoral responsibility that belongs to any "classic" read in a theologically serious interpretive community. First, I propose that seeing these texts as a *past* pertinent to the *present*, even if now suppressed or denied, permits the interpretive community to see fully who YHWH has been and potentially is. There is no cover-up of who this God is, no notion that this character can be made to conform to our preferred Enlightenment or orthodox categories of reading. A "second naïveté" permits the reading community to take this God with theological seriousness in all of YHWH's consternating Jewishness, in all of YHWH's refusal of domestication.

Second, if this character is understood as a real live agent who concerns the life of the reader or the reading community, the reader is thereby authorized and permitted to entertain "dark" dimensions of one's own life (or one's community) as palpable theological dimensions of reality. Both canonical and critical reading that fends off the "dark" texts encourages denial and cover-up of the intimate savageness of life. But when the reading community can see that brutality, abusiveness, and abandonment are alive and present in the past of this God, it is credible to take the same dimension in one's own life as past realities that continue to have potential power in the present.

It is not at all my intention to take a therapeutic or instrumental approach to the character of YHWH. Nonetheless, theological, interpretive, textual candor does have important pastoral consequences. The only way beyond such woundedness is through such woundedness. That ancient woundedness persists in text and in life. When voiced and accepted, as the text invites us to do, that ancient woundedness is robbed of its present lethal authority. As long as one pretends that these texts are not "back there," a terrible denial is required, which denies movement into a healing present and a healed future.

CHAPTER 8

Concerning Secondary Resources

THE DISCUSSIONS IN THIS BOOK WILL INDICATE THAT, IN MY OPINION, the best read of biblical text is a *direct, hands-on exploration of the internal rhetoric* of the particular text. For a very long time during the days of the hegemony of historical criticism, very much critical Scripture study did not read biblical texts, but only read *about* biblical texts or, in an even more remote way, read primarily about historical contexts that were taken as the lead clue to the intent of the text itself. The methodological "turn" in Scripture study toward *rhetorical criticism* and toward a *social-scientific approach* that viewed texts as arenas of interpretation contestation, turned attention to the text itself.[1] That in turn has become a primary preoccupation of current Scripture reading, in the academy as in church.

By attempting *a direct, hands-on exposition of the internal dynamics* of a text, I mean to suggest that one does not need to control a huge critical apparatus in order to read responsibly, as was mostly assumed in the older methods of historical criticism. Thus much of my teaching has been to empower students to have enough courage and imagination to go at a text, and to be surprised by the text in a way that allows a genuine "revealing" not known ahead of time.[2] One can learn a great deal by close attentiveness to the text, and that is the way the text has characteristically been read in the church.

1. On rhetorical criticism, see Phyllis Trible, *Rhetorical Criticism*. Though there are a rich variety of resources on social-scientific methods, the breakthrough study was that of Norman K. Gottwald, *The Tribes of Yahweh*.

2. By the term "revealing," I intend to suggest that the text is "revelatory," but not in any conventional scholastic sense. Rather, the revealing concerns that which is not known or seen or heard until the utterance of this particular text.

But that does not mean that one should be intellectually thin and rely exclusively on one's own judgments and impressions in a way that can too easily become solipsistic. It is wise to have available secondary sources that create a much wider horizon in which texts are to be understood. As the work of historical criticism has always assumed, attention to a wider horizon of data will protect from a thin ideological reading that only echoes back one's prejudices and interests. To that end, I will consider four strands of secondary sources that can be useful for reading responsibly in the church.

Language, History, Archaeology

It is necessary for responsible interpretation to have a broad base of knowledge concerning the cultural, historical context in which biblical texts are situated. Texts are never in a vacuum but are always generated by and reflective of cultural context. And a disregard of that context can lead to the misfortune of misreading. Awareness of context, of course, is no guarantee about responsible reading, but it is an essential resource:

Of necessity one wants to have a broad and informed sense of historical sequence, the rise and fall of power and the imperial context of the Ancient Near East, for the community of ancient Israel was always in the shadow of the empire and regularly impinged upon by the empire in defining ways.[3] Good resources for history and culture include Miller and Hayes, *A History of Ancient Israel and Judah*.[4] For Mesopotamia and Egypt, a great overview is available in Hallo and Simpson's *The Ancient Near East*.[5]

When possible, it is useful to have a working knowledge of Hebrew in order to have access to the impressionistic way of Hebrew rhetoric. This is a valuable resource, even if one's actual "working knowledge" is lean. Any exposure at all to the language can make a difference in what one

---

3. See Brueggemann, "Always in the Shadow of the Empire." Recent attention to postcolonial interpretation reflects an awareness of how the "shadow of empire" impinges upon our contemporary interpretation. See Rieger, *Christ and Empire*; Schüssler Fiorenza, *The Power of the Word: Scripture and the Rhetoric of Empire*; and Horsley, *Jesus and Empire*.

4. Miller and Hayes, *A History of Ancient Israel and Judah*. For a somewhat more conservative tilt, see Provan, Long, and Longman, *A Biblical History of Israel*.

5. Hallo and Simpson, *The Ancient Near East: A History*.

notices and how one reads. A lack of Hebrew knowledge, however, need not be a discouragement for faithful reading. Slow, steady, attentiveness to the English can make available a great deal in the text if one concerns the dynamic rhetorical power of the text and is not preoccupied with the interpretive "outcomes" of concepts, ideas, or propositions. Attention to the text may guard against the common reductionism of Enlightenment reading, either fundamentalist or critical.

Along with history and language, important background resources include archaeological data and the current interpretation of that data. Unless one has peculiar talents and skills in this area, one must rely upon the "experts." Such a study in archaeology in relationship to the Bible at the present time is filled with dramatic tension, as the confidence of an earlier generation of interpreters in relating the Bible to archaeological data is now profoundly shaken. One must take into account so-called "minimalist" interpretation of the data that has concluded that the "facts" of archaeology do not support many of the historical claims of the Bible. Perhaps the best guide is that of William G. Dever, even though his work is filled with polemics in many directions.[6] His recent books provide a summary of the data and, for the most part, offer balanced judgments that are widely respected in the field. The volumes in the Anchor Bible Reference Library, by Amihai Mazar and Ephraim Stern respectively, provide important systematic treatments of each archaeological era.[7]

With a general purview of history, language, and archaeology, an informed interpreter of the Bible might, like the leading scholars, pay particular attention to the great crisis moments in the faith of Israel, for those historical crises characteristically also represented theological crises. Thus major attention belongs to the founding crisis of Israel (Moses, Joshua), the establishment crisis (David, Solomon), and the disestablishment crisis (exile, displacement, and deportation).[8] After one has learned the sequence of historical events, it is evident that the remembered pivotal interpretive

6. Dever, *What Did the Biblical Writers Know and When Did They Know It?*; and idem, *Who Were the Early Israelites and Where Did They Come From?*

7. Mazar, *Archaeology of the Land of the Bible*, vol. 1; Stern, *Archaeology of the Land of the Bible*, vol. 2.

8. We will, in the process, recognize that these "historical crises" are enormously problematic from a critical perspective. Given that problematic, the articulation of these crises in the biblical text nonetheless attests to Israel's self-understanding and to its characteristic practice of tradition and interpretation.

points in the life of Israel evoked the most daring and most compelling theological testimony as well. For two approaches to history and memory, see the works of Mark S. Smith[9] and Yosef Hayim Yerushalmi.[10] There is important literature about those crises points to which attention must be paid, even though many matters continue to be in dispute about those crisis occasions. Concerning the founding crisis, still the best general orientation is that of Norman K. Gottwald, even though his defining work continues to be critiqued as well as refined.[11] The crisis of the monarchy has attracted great attention, as it reflects a consolidation of power that in broad stroke contradicted the defining covenantal memories and traditions of Israel. Reference will usefully be made to the work of Frank S. Frick and Marvin L. Chaney.[12]

A subset of the monarchal development in Israel is a consideration of the prophetic movement, for the prophets were voices of criticism and alternative vis-à-vis royal concentrations of power. Robert R. Wilson has provided standard sociological categories through which to situate the prophetic figures of ancient Israel in the maelstrom of power politics.[13] And Thomas W. Overholt provides both anthropological and communication models for understanding the prophetic dynamic.[14]

Concerning the sixth-century crisis of displacement and deportation, Daniel Smith-Christopher has provided an access point from which to consider those who were geographically relocated and those who remained in the land.[15] In every case it is evident that historical understanding provides an important matrix for theological interpretation.

9. Mark S. Smith, *The Memoirs of God.*

10. Yerushalmi, *Zakhor: Jewish History and Jewish Memory.*

11. Gottwald, *The Tribes of Yahweh.*

12. Frick, *The Formation of the State in Ancient Israel*; and Chaney, "Systemic Study of the Israelite Monarchy."

13. Wilson, *Prophecy and Society in Ancient Israel.*

14. Overholt, *Channels of Prophecy.*

15. Daniel L. Smith, *The Religion of the Landless: The Social Context of the Babylonian Exile*; Daniel L. Smith-Christopher, *Biblical Theology of Exile.* See also Jon L. Berquist, *Judaism in Persia's Shadow: A Social and Historical Approach.*

Introduction to the Old Testament

When one has a sense of the *historical context and sequence* of the biblical materials together with an awareness of the critical assessment of those biblical materials, one may draw closer to the text itself. The best way to do that is to have an "introduction," which in Old Testament studies tends to proceed "book by book" from Genesis to Malachi or, in Jewish sequence, from Genesis to 2 Chronicles. It is important to have a sense of "the book" as the primary location and context for a particular text, for the part must be read in terms of the whole.

In current Old Testament study, there are two tasks of introduction that merit attention. First, there is the *critical task*, a study of scholarly judgments about how the several books of the Bible are put together. There is any number of such introductory books now, but I suggest that a particularly useful heavyweight is the new introduction of John J. Collins.[16] He has also offered an abridged version.[17] A brief, multi-authored introduction is edited by Marti J. Steussy.[18] These books, and many others like them, state what is roughly a consensus in scholarship even though interpretive matters are greatly in flux.

The second task of interpretation—more important for church interpreters—is what has come to be called a "canonical" approach. That way of coming at the biblical text is primarily interested in theological rather than historical-critical questions. The defining study in this direction is the highly influential and enormously important study of Brevard S. Childs.[19] In his book of 1979 he reviews the critical data for each book of the Old Testament and then makes bold suggestions about how each book of the Old Testament is shaped decisively through self-aware theological intentionality. Some elements of Childs's proposal work better than others, but his study is enormously suggestive for serious theological interpreters. The main drawback of his book is that it is now almost thirty years old. A great deal has happened since then in interpretation, though much of it is informed primarily by his work. My own introduction of 2003 is much influenced by Childs and also pays attention to the canonical-theological

---

16. Collins, *Introduction to the Hebrew Bible*.

17. Collins, *A Short Introduction to the Hebrew Bible*.

18. Steussy, ed., *Chalice Introduction to the Old Testament*.

19. Childs, *Introduction to the Old Testament as Scripture*.

intention of the text.[20] There is some tension between approaches that are *canonical* and *critical*. It is clear, nonetheless, that responsible interpretation must work with both perspectives. Childs's model, now replicated by other scholars, is a major effort in taking critical questions seriously and moving on to canonical dimensions.

Concordance, Commentary, and Bible Dictionary

When one draws closer to specific texts, there are three tools that are indispensable. By all odds, the most important tool for interpretive methods as I have proposed them is a concordance. The value of a concordance is the ability to look up other uses of the same word, because rhetorical analysis assumes an inter-textual transaction in which texts are drawn into context and conversation with each other. Any concordance is usable, but it is highly preferable to have an "analytical" concordance, that is, a listing of words according to the Hebrew, Aramaic, and Greek "originals."[21] Without this analytic specificity one can make mistakes by citing two words translated by the same English term that in fact are renderings of different words in the "original." If one does not have an analytical concordance, one can still benefit by studying semantic fields, even if the words do not all render the same original word.

The second major resource for close textual work is the commentary. A church interpreter will want to have, if possible, several sets of commentaries available. Since different commentary series have different goals and intentions, one must select carefully, even while one is aware that within any commentary series work varies in value from volume to volume. The most technical commentaries are *Hermeneia* (Fortress Press)[22] and *The Anchor Bible* (Doubleday)[23] that focus on linguistic and

20. Brueggemann, *An Introduction to the Old Testament: The Canon and Christian Imagination*.

21. The most complete analytical concordance to the RSV is Whitaker, ed., *The Eerdmans Analytical Concordance to the Revised Standard Version of the Bible*. The old reliables, based on the King James Version, are Young, *Analytical Concordance to the Bible*; and Strong, *The New Strong's Exhaustive Concordance of the Bible*.

22. *Hermeneia: A Critical and Historical Commentary on the Bible*; the chair of the Old Testament Editorial Board was formerly Frank Moore Cross and is now Peter Machinist.

23. *The Anchor Bible*; the editor is David Noel Freedman, recently deceased.

philological analysis and other critical questions. These commentaries are of enormous value, but they do not—and do not intend—to offer theological exposition that goes very far toward contemporary communities of faith. For more direct church usage, two commentary series from Westminster John Knox are especially important: *The Westminster Bible Companion*[24] and *Interpretation*.[25] These offer theological insight that is more readily in the service of theological exposition. Occupying a middle position between the technical and the more popular is the *Old Testament Library*, also from Westminster John Knox, which has for a very long time been the most normative and representative of current scholarship. In this series as new volumes are issued, one can trace a movement from historical-critical study that was the strong focus of earlier volumes toward theological and rhetorical interest in more recent volumes. There are a variety of other commentaries, but I mention two others. The *Berit Olam* (Michael Glazier/Liturgical Press)[26] engages in more experimental methods, approaching the text in quite fresh ways. Finally, *The New Interpreters Bible* (Abingdon Press)[27] is among the best commentaries we have for church interpreters with a self-conscious delivery of theological dimension in each unit of the commentary. In the Classified Lists of Readings, the reader will also find several one-volume commentaries that are handy desktop volumes.

One other note about two new commentary series. There is now a great interest in recovering the "pre-critical" interpretive tradition of the church, that is, interpretation done before the modern period of historical criticism. *The Church's Bible* offers a rich sample of such early reading of texts,[28] as does a similar series, *Ancient Christian Commentary on Scripture*.[29] Obviously such a commentary must be used wisely (as is the case with every commentary), for the early church read texts in a way that was inherently supersessionist, and care must be taken about such preempting of Old Testament texts. At the pivot point between pre-critical

24. *The Westminster Bible Companion*; the Old Testament editor is Patrick D. Miller.

25. *Interpretation: A Bible Commentary for Teaching and Preaching*; the Old Testament editor is Patrick D. Miller.

26. *Berit Olam*; the Old Testament editor is Jerome T. Walsh.

27. *The New Interpreter's Bible*, edited by Leander E. Keck.

28. The first volume to be issued in the series is Robert Louis Wilken, *Isaiah: Interpreted by Early Christian and Medieval Commentators*.

29. *Ancient Christian Commentary on Scripture*, edited by Thomas C. Oden.

and critical, I may mention the commentaries of John Calvin, as well as those by Martin Luther. Calvin's and Luther's interpretations are rich with theological insight.

I add this note about commentaries. They are of great usefulness; it is important that commentaries should not be a substitute for working with the text for oneself, for the text is invariably more interesting and more demanding than any commentary.

A third resource is reference Bibles and dictionaries of the Bible. There are a variety of these to which attention must be paid. The most comprehensive study of historical matters is in the six-volume *Anchor Bible Dictionary*.[30] Two briefer volumes are *Eerdmans Dictionary of the Bible*,[31] and *Harper's Bible Commentary*.[32]

Reading Beyond Scripture

To these more obvious and more immediate secondary resources for Scripture interpretation, I add one other category of resources that does not normally occur in such an inventory, namely, reading beyond scripture in a way that considers contemporary currents in culture and society. Biblical interpretation never happens in a vacuum; church interpretation, moreover, has a mandate to interact with cultural emergents, both to find critical interfaces and to identify allies in a missional task. This interface, put most boldly, is a replay of the ancient interface between "Jerusalem and Athens," that is, between faith traditions and cultural learning. The possibilities for such reading (and electronic alternatives) is nearly limitless, and is certainly well beyond the time or energy of any church interpreter I know. Thus one must be disciplined and intentional about such reading and study.

It is important to have *journals* available that relate directly to the world of theological reflection and to the contemporary task of ministry. Most obviously this might include *Christian Century* and/or *Christianity Today*. The two of these twinned together may keep one from committing too easily to any simplistic ideological strand. For Scripture study more directly, a most useful resource is *Interpretation* (Union Theological

---

30. Freedman, ed., *Anchor Bible Dictionary*, 6 vols.
31. Freedman, ed., *Eerdmans Dictionary of the Bible*.
32. Achtemeier, ed. *Harper's Bible Dictionary*.

Seminary, Richmond, Virginia), which offers especially good book reviews. More broadly, I believe that the best journal for theological reflection is *Theology Today* (Princeton Theological Seminary), though attention may also be given to the more conservative *First Things*.

Beyond the closer realm of theological reflection a good Scripture reader may want to have available an opinion journal such as *Harpers* or *Atlantic* or *The Nation*. These journals reflect current thought and provide conversation partners for our own interpretive undertakings.

In addition to journal reading, there are two kinds of reading that seem to me most important. On the one hand, one might commit to "keeping up" in one or two intellectual disciplines. Given current interest in environmental issues and/or "science and religion," one might pay attention to the literature in scientific thought that is available to those who live and think outside scientific precision. Alternatively, one might work with some of the social sciences or literary criticism; indeed, any ongoing intellectual discussion that invites one outside what can be the parochial world of church interpretation. To that end, I quote Cornelius Plantinga Jr. who offers a continuing education course on "imaginative reading for creative preaching":

> People often assume that preachers who read widely are on the prowl for illustrations. These people are right. Preachers are hunter-gatherers; they search not only the world's literary masterworks, but also contemporary middle-brow fiction, crime journalism, and biography, hoping to dig up fresh and angular illustrations. But preachers are not merely in search of useful stories. Reading deepens the preacher's knowledge of human cries of the heart— for example that we reap what we sow. In fact, the preacher's reading deepens preaching because it deepens the preacher. The preacher, who presumes to speak for God or even for the church, has to struggle every day to understand human character, divine grace, and the surprises that gather at their intersection. To do so faithfully, most preachers will need the kind of vicarious experience that arises from immersion in well-chosen literature.[33]

On the other hand, "imaginative reading" may also include novels, poetry, and most especially, biography. In addition to the substance of such artistic enterprises, one may benefit greatly from exposure to the high craft of words, images, metaphors, and phrasing, for it is the work of

---

33. Announcement for Continuing Education event at Calvin Seminary.

scripture (and derivatively, of church interpretation) to "render the world" in fresh and transformative ways. Secondary resources function primarily not to provide "information" for church interpreters. They function to fund the imagination, deepen the perception, and thicken the courage of the interpreter who may then interpret with a great depth of awareness. In the end, after all the resources are mobilized, what still remains is an act of obedient imagination that matters in mediating true words of life in contemporary venues of life or death decision-making.[34]

34. On the interplay of obedience and imagination, see Brueggemann, *Interpretation and Obedience: From Faithful Reading to Faithful Living.*

CHAPTER 9

Conclusion: Interpretive Outcomes

IN THE END ONE MUST ASK ABOUT INTERPRETIVE METHOD IN TERMS of interpretive outcomes. If one is primarily committed to the historical accuracy of ancient texts, then historical criticism is pivotal for interpretation. One cannot, in any case, forego facing such historical questions. If, however, one understands *the transformative potential* of the text *as Scripture*, then one must move past historical questions into some sense of the contemporaneity of the text as generative and revelatory.[1] That move beyond historical to contemporary concerns is an important one, but it is also a profoundly hazardous one.[2] It is hazardous because every attempt at imaginative contemporaneity is obviously open to ideological tilt. Such a move can only be done responsibly after rigorous criticism; thus Ricoeur well understood that the "second naiveté" does not stand in close continuity with the "first naiveté," but is profoundly disrupted by criticism.[3] That criticism concerns not only the problematic historical claim of the text, important as that problematic is, but beyond that recent criticism has focused on the ideological propensity of the text, notably concerning

1. The present emphasis on taking the Bible "as Scripture" is singularly the gain made for us by Brevard S. Childs, *Introduction to the Old Testament as Scripture*. He has continued to underscore that angle of reading in a stream of important publications.

2. The move away from criticism to canon is central to Childs's work. But the push to the contemporary, a primary concern of mine, has not been of importance to Childs. He has left that work to others, even though he has no doubt that canon as Scripture makes contemporary claims. He does not go very far in showing how he thinks this works.

3. See Wallace, *The Second Naiveté*. There is currently great energy in the recovery of pre-critical exegesis, that is, in the first naiveté. See Byassee, *Praise Seeking Understanding*; and Wilken, *Isaiah: Interpreted by Early Church and Medieval Commentators*.

violence, patriarchy, ethnicity, and a dozen other temptations to channel theological claims toward special pleading.[4]

Elisabeth Schüssler Fiorenza has summarized all of these tempting ideological claims under the recognition that "empire" is deeply "inscribed" in the text; it is therefore not at all surprising that "empire" is "inscribed" in much of our interpretation.[5] I do notice, as a point of hope, that Joerg Rieger has suggested that in the midst of empire there occurs regularly a "surplus" of gospel that is not fully contained in or domesticated by empire.[6] I suppose that it is "surplus" that still provides the possibility that the text can be received as generative and revelatory.

Three Eighteenth-Century Options

In the eighteenth century, seedbed of my particular interpretive trajectory, as I have noted, the available interpretive options in Germanic Protestantism were limited to three. *Orthodoxy* was a scholastic reductionism of Reformation faith that arrived at a package of propositional certitudes concerning the substance of faith. Such a scholasticism inevitably and inescapably evoked a response of *rationalism* that resisted the high-handed authoritarianism of faith rendered as proposition, and sought to establish rational grounds for faith and to limit faith claims to "the reasonable." It is this response to orthodox scholasticism that evoked historical criticism in the academic community, a criticism that in Old Testament studies produced the "Documentary Hypothesis" and in New Testament studies produced the "Quest for the Historical Jesus."

The practice in which I am rooted and which continues to propel my work in important ways sought to establish a more intimate mode of faith outside the temptations of orthodoxy and rationalism. This latter *pietism* affirmed the substance of faith but refused its reduction to proposition and expressed trust in an intimate relationship that could not be reduced to proposition. The temptation of such pietism became provincial moralism; at its best the tradition of pietism evoked a dependency upon God's

---

4. On that destructive potential in the textual tradition, see Schwartz, *The Curse of Cain: The Violent Legacy of Monotheism.*

5. Schüssler Fiorenza, *The Power of the Word: Scripture and the Rhetoric of Empire.*

6. Rieger, *Christ and Empire.*

graciousness that permitted a reading of Scripture not permeated by either the certitude of orthodoxy or the alternative certitude of rationalism.

Contemporary Options

I mention this interpretive triangle yet again because I believe it illuminates contemporary tensions in the interpretive process. The scholasticism of eighteenth-century orthodoxy continues to be present in every effort at a propositional certitude, an enterprise that has been aggressively pursued in the turmoil of Southern Baptist quarrels, in Missouri Synod Lutheranism, and in other denominational traditions as well. My impression about such a contemporary interpretive propensity is that it is evoked by the deep and broad anxiety rooted in a sense that the contemporary world is in jeopardy and under assault. Such a scholastic certitude is an attempt to find safety and security in some "settled truth." It is noteworthy, even if curious, that this kind of scholasticism, in many quarters, has in fact devolved into a negative concern about gays and lesbians in church and in society. Thus much of the current agitation about "the authority of Scripture" in fact is simply code talk for a particular position on issues of sexuality, obviously without regard to many other dimensions of Scripture that ought rightly to vex the church.

Alongside such contemporary scholasticism is what we might term contemporary rationalism that takes the preferred title of "*progressivism.*" Such an interpretive stance, not unlike eighteenth-century rationalism, wants to identify the core theological-ethical claims of biblical faith apart from the "mythological framing" of "supernaturalism" and the miracles that stand at the center of such claims. Contemporary rational-progressive interpretation wants to unburden the faith of much of the "surplus" freight of "Catholic Christianity" and get to the bare essentials of a revolutionary movement. While it is not always the case, it is noticeable enough to observe that much of the fuel for this movement is supplied by those who come out of conservative-authoritarian backgrounds of faith and have been wounded by a church (and church interpretation) that imposed interpretive outcomes without inviting anyone into the interpretive process.

The current tension in the church between conservative (orthodox) interpretation and liberal (rational) interpretation tends to parcel scripture out into its preferred elements. For such parceling out, my favorite descriptive phrase is that we are all "selective fundamentalists" who pick and choose a package of certitudes that will sustain a particular stance of faith and action in the world.

While my own social-ethical passions are completely on the side of the "progressives," it is unmistakably clear to me that so-called "progressives" who hold for "liberal Christianity" have not much sustained interest in the testimony of Scripture itself, for Scripture does not lend itself to any simplistic outcome. For that reason, I attempt to practice interpretation that is in informed by criticism (the standing ground of liberal progressives) and by the conviction and appeal of traditionalists, but I am not fully persuaded by either. Thus without interest in labels, I find myself practicing what has come to be called post-modernist or post-foundationalist interpretation. In these labels, the "post" is especially important.[7] "Post" as in "post-modern" means after complete confidence in rational criticism. "Post" as in "post-foundationalism" means that we cannot appeal to settled universal truth, but that the testimony of Scripture and of any particular scriptural texts must be taken on its own terms for what it is, without making too grand a claim for it.[8] I believe that Scripture interpretation, in the church, is a gift for the day, and the gift is to be received that day, but must be done all over again the next day. Such resistance to "canonical" or "objective" or "settled truth," of course, smacks of "relativism." But then any reading of the text or exposition of it is inescapably related to context and therefore our interpretive claims must be modest and, I believe, tentative in any particular. I believe that any such practice is congruent with and congenial to the dialogic process that constitutes authentic human engagement with the disclosures of the dialogical God of the text.[9] This way of doing interpretation thus insists upon a dialogical transaction of text and reader, text and community, text from the past and from past existence in the world.

While I have suggested interesting connections between eighteenth-century orthodoxy and contemporary conservatism and eighteenth-century rationalism and contemporary progressivism, I want now to suggest a quite provisional connection between eighteenth-century pietism and contemporary post-modern interpretation. It is clear that any con-

7. See Brueggemann, "The Re-emergence of Scripture: Post-Liberalism."

8. For access to these issues, see Thiel, *Nonfoundationalism*.

9. For an introduction to such a dialogical enterprise by way of the originary work of Martin Buber, see Steven Kepnes, *The Text as Thou: Martin Buber's Dialogical Hermeneutics and Narrative Theology*.

nection of contemporary to older practice must be tentative and provisional. The connection I suggest is that contemporary post-foundational interpretation must be modest and "innocent" and rooted in a kind of naïveté that in ancient time and in present time must be of a "second" sort.

An Alternative Imagination

Thus I suggest my own location in interpretation and the more general discussion of contemporary interpretation has important connections with older practices. The post-modern perspective that is embodied in the methods of these essays is an attempt to read and hear outside the rational assumptions of dominant society and outside the hegemonic claims of established church practice. Such an attempt—that can never be more than partial—is an attempt to articulate and enact an alternative imagination, that is, a construal of reality that is not contained with either dominant rational assumptions or dominant church authority. It means to let the text deliver an alternative scenario of reality that has as its defining force the central character of God before whom all else must be altered. The proposed reality, with God at its center, is clearly alternative to dominant societal reality and, for the most part, dominant church reality, for in neither is the agency of God very central or powerful in telling the narrative of the world.

This alternative imagination that is voiced in Scripture—albeit not without its crippling defects—is indeed alternative to the way we generally take the world to be. In the immediate context where I live, it is alternative to the imperial reality of the United States together with all of the social and personal pathologies that are fostered by the imperatives of empire. The alternative—which follows an alternative reading of reality—declares to be possible what dominant reality characteristically has declared to be impossible.

An Alternative World

This way of reading the text invites us to a construal of reality that is not trimmed back to "the reason of this age." In this alternative world of impossible possibility:

- the world is framed as creation (not nature) and culminates in the "Kingdom of God" (not burned up or frozen over);

- the world is permeated with miracles, notably exodus emancipations and resurrections to new life;

- the character of God is one who judges a world that takes itself to be autonomous and who restores a world that thought itself mired in despair;

- the world is sustained as a morally coherent creation that is alternative to a "dog-eat-dog" contest for survival.

Scripture thus renders a world that refuses to stay within the sober bounds of "orthodoxy" or that refuses to submit to the reason of this age. Scripture renders such a world, and we who interpret are invited to a project of echoing Scripture and giving voice to a reality other than the one that is readily available to us. Because this reading of reality violates our readiest assumptions, it is no surprise that such a reading is always a scandal. Even given its quality of scandal, we nevertheless gather around the script to hear words again, from which we speak words of exposition and interpretation. We commit the audacious act in interpretation of moving from the word given to the words we speak. We do so, properly, with modesty and humility, because we are kept aware that our best words are not the words given in Scripture. Our words, only in a derivative way, can claim to mediate what is revelatory. The slippage between *the word given* and *the words we utter* is so great that we do better not to speak interpretation at all.[10] Except that we cannot help ourselves, because there is something shut up in silence "like a burning fire" (Jer 5:14). Thus we take on the jeopardizing task of speaking when we had best keep silent. I repeat Karl Barth's aphorism, which is exactly right:

> . . . here we are discussing our common *situation*. This situation I will characterize in the three following sentences: —*As ministers we ought to speak of God. We are human, however, and so cannot speak of God. We ought therefore to recognize both* our obligation and our inability *and by that very recognition give God the glory.*

10. The inescapable slippage between the "word given" and the "word uttered" is made explicit in Jeremiah 1:1-2 with the distinction between "the words of Jeremiah" and "the word of YHWH." This candid acknowledgment of the distinction is a crucial one for all of our interpretive work.

This is our perplexity. The rest of our task fades into insignificance in comparison.[11]

Entrusted with Words

We interpreters are in the word business. We study words; we hear words. We are given words, and we speak words. The word that is entrusted to us that we speak is not God's word. It is, rather, our interpreting word, summoning our best interpretation, a reliable word but a word impinged upon by our honest fears, our interests, and our hurts.

What a marvel to have these words given and entrusted to us! Because it is by words that we become and remain human. At its best, human existence is a communal act of conversation by which we endlessly empower and summon each other.

To be entrusted with words in our society is an awesome vocation. Jacques Ellul has written of the "humiliation of the word," by which he refers to the triumphant technology that produces *images* of reality that have immense staying power vis-à-vis the fleeting career of words uttered and heard.[12] In an image-propelled society that silences much of what is most dangerous and contested among us, words have a very hard time of it. James Boyd White has reflected on the way in which "free speech" is the language of commerce and trade where everything is reduced to commodity.[13] We need only think of the techno-speech of military discourse in which everything is given in a passive voice without responsible agency or psychobabble in which reality is reduced to radical subjectivity. White cites numerous cases of such "free speech" that are empty of human power or seriousness, utterances that have become the parlance of a commoditized society. Such commoditization is evident in sports and in politics, and is a sore temptation to the church.

In the face of such "free speech" White reflects on the capacity of "living speech," utterance in which human agents address each other in empowerment and summons that generates human possibility. It is always a decision, I submit, for biblical interpreters and church utterers to speak in the form of "free speech" that gives or requires nothing human, or "living

11. Barth, *The Word of God and the Word of Man*, 186.
12. Ellul, *The Humiliation of the Word*.
13. White, *Living Speech: Resisting the Empire of Force*.

speech" that generates a vision of the possible that evokes a community of faithful practice. We may take Jeremiah, with fire in his bones, as an exemplar embodiment of living speech.[14] Perhaps we can evidence his living speech by his capacity to generate hope and social possibility. But before that, we may test his speech by the way he regularly collides with authorities in his society, wherein he is regarded as an enemy for his own hometown people (Jer 11:21), wherein he senses "terror on every side" (Jer 20:10), wherein his scroll is shredded as subversive (Jer 36:23), and wherein he is accused as a traitor (Jer 38:4). His living speech consists of truth-telling, hope-telling acts that are unbearable in a commoditized society.

By contrast, the opponents of Jeremiah, notably Hananiah, have no words given to them but "speak visions of their own minds" (Jer 23:16). In such utterance they give phony assurance in the face of ominous social reality:

> They have treated the wound of my people carelessly,
>
> saying, "Peace, peace," when there is no peace. (Jer 6:14; see 8:11)

Such "free speech," always a temptation among us, seduces and bewitches but finally deceives. In the end, whatever we may make of criticism and/or second naiveté, the task of interpretation is living speech, a truth-telling utterance that summons listeners to face "the plucking up and the tearing down" that invites listeners to anticipate "the planting and the building" (Jer 1:10). Free speech can come easily in our society of denial and fate us to despair. But living speech offers *truth against denial* and *hope against despair*. Such utterance is a tall order for a Scripture interpreter.

None of us would do it were we on our own. We are entrusted with a text and we dare to notice that the entire process of the text, from formation and transmission to our own faithful interpretation is indeed spirit led. Given all the images that dominate our social experience, it is nonetheless the case that people will wait for primary speech. They wait for a story, a song, or a poem that, in all its particularity, mediates holy power among us. By the time we understand ourselves as such interpreters—rendering story, song, and poem—we are well past conventional critical questions. We are at the edge of a rawness where holiness touches

---

14. See my explication of these themes in Brueggemann, *Like Fire in the Bones: Listening for the Prophetic Word in Jeremiah*.

and evokes humanness. Every interpreter faces the seduction of making things normal, routine, and business as usual. When we are alert to the risk of living speech, there is nothing normal or routine or business as usual about the task of interpretation. Every time we entertain the task of interpretation we find it to be a life-or-death matter, exactly what we would expect with a text that we have found to be thickly revelatory.

A CLASSIFIED READING LIST

Study Bibles

Attridge, Harold W., editor. *HarperCollins Study Bible*. Rev. ed. San Francisco: Harper-SanFrancisco, 2006.

Berlin, Adele, and Marc Zvi Brettler, editors. *The Jewish Study Bible: Jewish Publication Society Tanakh Translation*. New York: Oxford University Press, 2004.

Coogan, Michael David, editor. *The New Oxford Annotated Bible with the Apocrypha/Deuterocanonical Books*. 3rd ed. Oxford: Oxford University Press, 2007.

Harrelson, Walter, editor. *The New Interpreter's Study Bible: New Revised Standard Version with Apocrypha*. Nashville: Abingdon, 2003.

Senior, Donald, editor. *The Catholic Study Bible*. New York: Oxford University Press, 1990.

Concordances

Strong, James. *The New Strong's Exhaustive Concordance of the Bible*. Nashville: Nelson, 1984.

Whitaker, Richard E. *The Eerdmans Analytical Concordance to the Revised Standard Version of the Bible*. Grand Rapids: Eerdmans, 1988.

Young, Robert. *Analytical Concordance to the Bible*. Nashville: Abingdon, 1982.

Bible Dictionaries

Achtemeier, Paul J., editor. *HarperCollins Bible Dictionary*. San Francisco: HarperSan-Francisco, 1996.

Freedman, David Noel, editor. *The Anchor Bible Dictionary*. 6 vols. New York: Doubleday, 1992.

———, editor. *Eerdmans Bible Dictionary*. Grand Rapids: Eerdmans, 2000.

Biblical Interpretation

Barton, John, editor. *Cambridge Companion to Biblical Interpretation*. Cambridge Companions to Religion. Cambridge: Cambridge University Press, 1998.

———. *Reading the Old Testament: Method in Biblical Studies*. Philadelphia: Westminster, 1984.

Brueggemann, Walter. *The Bible Makes Sense*. Rev. ed. Louisville: Westminster John Knox, 2001.

Collins, John J. *The Bible after Babel: Historical Criticism in a Postmodern Age*. Grand Rapids: Eerdmans, 2005.

Coote, Robert B., and Mary P. Coote. *Power, Politics, and the Making of the Bible*. Minneapolis: Fortress, 1990.

Gillingham, Susan E., editor. *One Bible, Many Voices: Different Approaches to Biblical Study*. Grand Rapids: Eerdmans, 1999.

Levenson, Jon D. *The Hebrew Bible, the Old Testament, and Historical Criticism: Jews and Christians in Biblical Studies*. Louisville: Westminster John Knox, 1993.

McKenzie, Steven L., and Stephen R. Haynes, editors. *To Each Its Own Meaning: An Introduction to Biblical Criticisms and Their Application*. Rev. ed. Louisville: Westminster John Knox, 1999.

Morgan, Robert, with John Barton. *Biblical Interpretation*. Oxford Bible Series. New York: Oxford University Press, 1988.

Perdue, Leo G., editor. *The Blackwell Companion to the Hebrew Bible*. Blackwell Companions to Religion 3. Malden, MA: Blackwell, 2001.

Ricoeur, Paul. *Essays on Biblical Interpretation*. Edited with an Introduction by Lewis S. Mudge. Philadelphia: Fortress, 1980.

Rogerson, John, et al. *Beginning Old Testament Study*. Rev. ed. St. Louis: Chalice, 1998.

Sawyer, John F. A., editor. *The Blackwell Companion to the Bible and Culture*. Blackwell Companions to Religion. Malden, MA: Blackwell, 2006.

Introduction to the Old Testament

Brueggemann, Walter. *An Introduction to the Old Testament: The Canon and Christian Imagination*. Louisville: Westminster John Knox, 2003.

Collins, John J. *Introduction to the Hebrew Bible*. Minneapolis: Fortress, 2004.

———. *A Short Introduction to the Hebrew Bible*. Minneapolis: Fortress, 2007.

Gottwald, Norman K. *The Hebrew Bible: A Socio-Literary Introduction, with CD-ROM*. Philadelphia: Fortress, 1985, 2002.

Steussy, Marti J., editor. *Chalice Introduction to the Old Testament*. St. Louis: Chalice, 2003.

Archaeology and History

Coogan, Michael D., editor. *Oxford History of the Biblical World*. New York: Oxford University Press, 1998.

Dever, William G. *What Did the Biblical Writers Know and When Did They Know It? What Archaeology Can Tell Us about Ancient Israel*. Grand Rapids: Eerdmans, 2001.

——. *Who Were the Early Israelites and Where Did They Come From?* Grand Rapids: Eerdmans, 2003.

Hallo, William W., and William Kelly Simpson. *The Ancient Near East: A History*. 2nd ed. Fort Worth: Harcourt Brace College, 1998.

Isserlin, B. S. J. *The Israelites*. 1998. Reprinted, Minneapolis: Fortress, 2001.

Mazar, Amihai. *Archaeology of the Land of the Bible: 10,000 to 586 B.C.E.* Anchor Bible Reference Library. New York: Doubleday, 1990.

Miller, J. Maxwell, and John H. Hayes. *A History of Ancient Israel and Judah*. 2nd ed. Louisville: Westminster John Knox, 2006.

Stern, Ephraim. *Archaeology of the Land of the Bible*. Vol. 2: *The Assyrian, Babylonian, and Persian Periods, 732 to 332 B.C.E.* Anchor Bible Reference Library. New York: Doubleday, 2001.

Brief Bible Commentaries

Barton, John, and John Muddiman, editors. *The Oxford Bible Commentary*. Oxford: Oxford University Press, 2001.

Brown, Raymond E., et al., editors. *The New Jerome Biblical Commentary*. Englewood Cliffs, NJ: Prentice Hall, 1990.

Brueggemann, Walter, et al. *Texts for Preaching: A Lectionary Commentary, Based on the NRSV*. 3 vols. Louisville: Westminster John Knox, 1993–94.

Farmer, William R., editor. *The International Bible Commentary*. Collegeville, MN: Liturgical, 1998.

Mays, James L., editor. *The HarperCollins Bible Commentary*. San Francisco: HarperSanFrancisco, 2000.

Newsome, Carol, and Sharon Ringe, editors. *Women's Bible Commentary*. Expanded edition. Louisville: Westminster John Knox, 1998.

Rhetorical Criticism

Alter, Robert. *The Art of Biblical Narrative*. New York: Basic Books, 1981.

——. *The Art of Biblical Poetry*. New York: Basic Books, 1985.

——. *The David Story: A Translation with Commentary of 1 and 2 Samuel*. New York: Norton, 1999.

——. *The Five Books of Moses*. New York: Norton, 2004.

——. *The World of Biblical Literature*. New York: Basic Books, 1992.

Amit, Yairah. *Reading Biblical Narratives: Literary Criticism and the Hebrew Bible.* Minneapolis: Fortress, 2001.

Brueggemann, Walter. *The Covenanted Self: Explorations in Law and Covenant.* Edited by Patrick D. Miller. Minneapolis: Fortress, 1999.

———. *Genesis.* Interpretation. Atlanta: John Knox, 1982.

———. *The Message of the Psalms.* Augsburg Old Testament Studies. Minneapolis: Augsburg, 1984.

———. *Texts that Linger Words that Explode: Listening to Prophetic Voices.* Edited by Patrick D. Miller. Minneapolis: Fortress, 2000.

Clines, David J. A., David M. Gunn, and Alan J. Hauser, editors. *Art and Meaning: Rhetoric in Biblical Literature.* Journal for the Study of the Old Testament Supplement Series 19. Sheffield: Dept. of Biblical Studies, University of Sheffield, 1982.

Knierim, Rolf. "Criticism of Literary Features, Form, Tradition, and Redaction." In *The Hebrew Bible and Its Modern Interpreters,* edited by Douglas A. Knight and Gene M. Tucker, 123–65. The Bible and Its Modern Interpreters 1. Philadelphia: Fortress, 1985.

Muilenburg, James. *Hearing and Speaking the Word: Selections from the Works of James Muilenburg.* Scholars Press Homage Series. Chico, CA: Scholars, 1984.

Roth, W. M. W. "Rhetorical Criticism, Hebrew Bible." In *Dictionary of Biblical Interpretation.* 2 vols. Edited by John H. Hayes, 2:396–99. Nashville: Abingdon, 1999.

Trible, Phyllis. *God and the Rhetoric of Sexuality.* Overtures to Biblical Theology. Philadelphia: Fortress, 1978.

———. *Rhetorical Criticism: Context, Method, and the Book of Job.* Guides to Biblical Scholarship. Minneapolis: Fortress, 1994.

Watson, Duane F., and Alan J. Hauser, editors. *Rhetorical Criticism of the Bible: A Comprehensive Bibliography with Notes on History and Method.* Biblical Interpretation Series 4. Leiden: Brill, 1994.

Social Analysis

Bach, Alice, editor. *Women in the Hebrew Bible.* London: Routledge, 1999.

Brueggemann, Walter. *David's Truth: In Israel's Imagination and Memory.* 2nd ed. Minneapolis: Fortress, 2002.

———. "Old Testament Theology as a Particular Conversation: Adjudication of Israel's Sociotheological Alternatives." In *Old Testament Theology: Essays on Structure, Theme, and Text,* edited by Patrick D. Miller, 118–49. Minneapolis: Fortress, 1992.

———. "Scripture: Old Testament." In *The Blackwell Companion to Political Theology,* edited by Peter Scott and William T. Cavanaugh, 7–20. Blackwell Companions to Religion 6. Malden, MA: Blackwell, 2004.

———. *A Social Reading of the Old Testament: Prophetic Approaches to Israel's Communal Life.* Edited by Patrick D. Miller. Minneapolis: Fortress, 1994.

———. "The Transformative Potential of a Public Metaphor: Isaiah 37:21–29." In *Interpretation and Obedience: From Faithful Reading to Faithful Living*, 70–99. Minneapolis: Fortress, 1991.

Carter, Charles E., and Carol L. Meyers, editors. *Community, Identity, and Ideology. Sources for Biblical Theological Study* 6. Winona Lake, IN: Eisenbrauns, 1996.

Chaney, Marvin L. "Ancient Palestinian Peasant Movements and the Formation of Premonarchic Israel." In *Palestine in Transition: The Emergence of Ancient Israel*, edited by David Noel Freedman and David F. Graf, 39–90. The Social World of Biblical Antiquity Series 2. Sheffield: Almont, 1983.

———. "Bitter Bounty: The Dynamics of Political Economy Critiqued by the Eighth-Century Prophets." In *Reformed Faith and Economics*, edited by Robert L. Stivers, 15–30. Lanham, MD: University Press of America, 1989.

———. "Models Matter: Political Economy and Micah 6:9–15." In *Ancient Israel: The Old Testament in Its Social Context*, edited by Philip F. Esler, 145–60. Minneapolis: Fortress, 2006.

———. "Systemic Study of the Israelite Monarchy." *Semeia* 37 (1986) 53–76.

———. "Whose Sour Grapes? The Addressees of Isaiah 5:1–7 in the Light of Political Economy." *Semeia* 87 (1999) 105–22.

Clements, R. E., editor. *The World of Ancient Israel: Sociological, Anthropological, and Political Perspectives*. Cambridge: Cambridge University Press, 1989.

Esler, Philip F., editor. *Ancient Israel: The Old Testament in Its Social Context*. Minneapolis: Fortress, 2006.

Gottwald, Norman K. *The Hebrew Bible in Its Social World and Ours*. Semeia Studies. Atlanta: Scholars, 1993.

———. *The Politics of Ancient Israel*. Library of Ancient Israel. Louisville: Westminster John Knox, 2000.

———. *The Tribes of Yahweh: A Sociology of Liberated Israel, 1250–1050 B.C.E.* Maryknoll, NY: Orbis, 1979.

———, and Richard A. Horsley, editors. *The Bible and Liberation: Political and Social Hermeneutics*. Rev. ed. Bible and Liberation Series. Maryknoll, NY: Orbis, 1993.

Jobling, David, et al., editors. *The Bible and the Politics of Exegesis: Essays in Honor of Norman K. Gottwald on His Sixty-fifth Birthday*. Cleveland: Pilgrim, 1991.

Lang, Bernhard. *Monotheism and the Prophetic Minority: An Essay in Biblical History and Sociology*. Social World of Biblical Antiquity Series 1. Sheffield: Almond, 1983.

Meyers, Carol. *Discovering Eve: Ancient Israelite Women in Context*. Oxford: Oxford University Press, 1988.

———. *Households and Holiness: The Religious Culture of Israelite Women*. Facets. Minneapolis: Fortress, 2005.

———, editor. *Women in Scripture*. 2000. Reprinted, Grand Rapids: Eerdmans, 2001.

Overholt, Thomas W. *Channels of Prophecy: The Social Dynamics of Prophetic Activity*. Minneapolis: Fortress, 1989.

———. *Cultural Anthropology and the Old Testament*. Guides to Biblical Scholarship. Minneapolis: Fortress, 1996.

Pilch, John J., and Bruce J. Malina, editors. *Handbook of Biblical Social Values.* Peabody, MA: Hendrickson, 1998.

Smith-Christopher, Daniel L. *A Biblical Theology of Exile.* Overtures to Biblical Theology. Minneapolis: Fortress, 2002.

Theological Interpretation of Scripture

Barton, John. *Understanding Old Testament Ethics: Approaches and Explorations.* Louisville: Westminster John Knox, 2003.

Birch, Bruce C. *Let Justice Roll Down: The Old Testament, Ethics, and Christian Life.* Louisville: Westminster John Knox, 1991.

———, Walter Brueggemann, Terence Fretheim, and David L. Petersen. *A Theological Introduction to the Old Testament.* 2nd ed. Nashville: Abingdon, 2005.

Brueggemann, Walter. *The Book That Breathes New Life: Scriptural Authority and Biblical Theology.* Edited by Patrick D. Miller. Minneapolis: Fortress, 2005.

———. *Interpretation and Obedience: From Faithful Reading to Faithful Living.* Minneapolis: Fortress, 1991.

———. *Old Testament Theology: Essays on Structure, Theme, and Text.* Edited by Patrick D. Miller. Minneapolis: Fortress, 1992.

———. *Praying the Psalms.* 2nd ed. Eugene, OR: Cascade Books, 2006.

———. *Theology of the Old Testament: Testimony, Dispute, Advocacy.* Minneapolis: Fortress, 1997.

Childs, Brevard S. *Biblical Theology of the Old and New Testaments.* Minneapolis: Fortress, 1992.

———. *Introduction to the Old Testament as Scripture.* Philadelphia: Fortress, 1979.

Fowl, Stephen E. *Engaging Scripture: A Model for Theological Interpretation.* Challenges in Contemporary Theology. Malden, MA: Blackwell, 1998.

———, editor. *The Theological Interpretation of Scripture: Classic and Contemporary Readings.* Blackwell Readings in Modern Theology. Cambridge, MA: Blackwell, 1997.

———, and L. Gregory Jones. *Reading in Communion: Scripture and Ethics in Christian Life.* 1991. Reprinted, Eugene, OR: Wipf & Stock, 1998.

Gerstenberger, Erhard S. *Theologies in the Old Testament.* Translated by John Bowden. Minneapolis: Fortress, 2002.

Hanson, Paul D. *The Diversity of Scripture: A Theological Interpretation.* Overtures to Biblical Theology. Philadelphia: Fortress, 1982.

Seitz, Christopher, and Kathryn Greene-McCreight, editors. *Theological Exegesis: Essays in Honor of Brevard S. Childs.* Grand Rapids: Eerdmans, 1999.

Vanhoozer, Kevin J., editor. *Dictionary for Theological Interpretation of the Bible.* Grand Rapids: Baker Academic, 2005.

BIBLIOGRAPHY

Achtemeier, Paul J., editor. *HarperCollins Bible Dictionary.* San Francisco: HarperSan-Francisco, 1996.

Alter, Robert. *The Art of Biblical Narrative.* New York: Basic Books, 1981.

———. *The Art of Biblical Poetry.* New York: Basic Books, 1985.

Balthasar, Hans Urs von. *Theo-drama: Theological Dramatic Theory.* Vol. 1: *Prolegomena.* San Francisco: Ignatius, 1988.

———. *Theo-drama: Theological Dramatic Theory.* Vol. 2: *The Dramàtis Personae: Man in God.* San Francisco: Ignatius, 1990

Barr, James. *The Concept of Biblical Theology: An Old Testament Perspective.* Minneapolis: Fortress, 1999.

Barth, Karl. "The Strange New World within the Bible." In *The Word of God and the Word of Man,* 28–50. Translated by Douglas Horton. New York: Harper & Brothers, 1957.

———. *The Word of God and the Word of Man.* Translated by Douglas Horton. New York: Harper & Brothers, 1957.

Berger, Peter R., and Thomas Luckmann. *The Social Construction of Reality: A Treatise in the Sociology of Knowledge.* Garden City, NY: Doubleday, 1967.

Berquist, Jon L. *Judaism in Persia's Shadow: A Social and Historical Approach.* 1995. Reprinted, Eugene, OR: Wipf & Stock, 2002.

Blumenthal, David R. *Facing the Abusing God: A Theology of Protest.* Louisville: Westminster John Knox, 1993.

Bright, John. *The Early History of Israel in Recent History Writing.* Studies in Biblical Theology 19. Chicago: Allenson, 1956.

Brown, Dale. *The Book of Buechner: A Journey through His Writings.* Louisville: Westminster John Knox, 2006.

Brueggemann, Walter. "Always in the Shadow of the Empire." In *The Church as Counterculture,* edited by Michael L. Budde and Robert W. Brimlow, 39–58. Albany: SUNY Press, 2000.

———. *Biblical Perspectives on Evangelism: Living in a Three-Storied Universe.* Nashville: Abingdon, 1993.

———. "I Samuel 1: A Sense of a Beginning." *Zeitschrift für die alttestamentliche Wissenschaft* 102 (1990) 33–47.

———. "Genesis 50:15–20: A Theological Exploration." In *Congress Volume, Salamanca, 1983*, edited by J. A. Emerton, 40–53. Vetus Testamentum Supplements 36. Leiden: Brill, 1985; reprinted in Brueggemann, *Old Testament Theology: Essays on Structure, Theme, and Text*, edited by Patrick D. Miller, 204–18. Minneapolis: Fortress, 1991.

———. *Hopeful Imagination: Prophetic Voices in Exile*. Philadelphia: Fortress, 1986.

———. *Interpretation and Obedience: From Faithful Reading to Faithful Living*. Minneapolis: Fortress, 1991.

———. *An Introduction to the Old Testament: The Canon and Christian Imagination*. Louisville: Westminster John Knox, 2003.

———. "James. L. Crenshaw: Faith Lingering at the Edges." *Religious Studies Review* 20/2 (1994) 103–10.

———. *Like Fire in the Bones: Listening for the Prophetic Word in Jeremiah*. Minneapolis: Fortress, 2006.

———. *Old Testament Theology: Essays on Structure, Theme, and Text*. Edited by Patrick D. Miller. Minneapolis: Fortress, 1992.

———. "Preaching as Subversion." *Theology Today* 55 (1998) 195–212.

———. *The Prophetic Imagination*. Philadelphia: Fortress, 1978. 2nd ed. 2001.

———. "The Recovering God of Hosea." *Horizons in Biblical Theology*, forthcoming.

———. "The Re-emergence of Scripture: Post-Liberalism." In *The Bible in Pastoral Practice: Readings in the Place and Function of Scripture in the Church*, edited by Paul Ballard and Stephen R. Holmes, 153–73. London: Darton, Longman and Todd, 2005.

———. "A Shape of Old Testament Theology, I: Structure Legitimation." In *Old Testament Theology: Essays on Structure, Theme, and Text*, edited by Patrick D. Miller, 1–21. Minneapolis: Fortress, 1992.

———. "Texts that Linger, Not Yet Overcome." In *Shall Not the Judge of All the Earth Do What is Right? Studies on the Nature of God in Tribute to James L. Crenshaw*, edited by David Penchansky and Paul L. Redditt, 21–41. Winona Lake, IN: Eisenbrauns, 2000) 21-41

———. *Texts That Linger, Words that Explode: Listening to Prophetic Voices*. Minneapolis: Fortress, 2000.

———. *Texts under Negotiation: The Bible and Postmodern Imagination*. Minneapolis: Fortress, 1993.

———. *Theology of the Old Testament: Testimony, Dispute, Advocacy*. Minneapolis: Fortress, 1997.

———. "Trajectories in Old Testament Literature and the Sociology of Ancient Israel." *Journal of Biblical Literature* 98 (1979) 161–85.

———. "Voice as Counter to Violence." *Calvin Theological Journal* 36 (2001) 22–33.

———. *The Word that Redescribes the World: The Bible and Discipleship*. Minneapolis: Fortress, 2006.

Buechner, Frederick. *Now and Then*. San Francisco: HarperSanFrancisco, 1991.

Byassee, Jason. *Praise Seeking Understanding: Reading the Psalms with Augustine*. Grand Rapids: Eerdmans, 2007.

Calvin, John. *Commentary on the Book of the Prophet Isaiah.* Calvin's Commentaries 8. Grand Rapids: Baker, 1979.

Childs, Brevard S. *Biblical Theology of the Old and New Testaments: Theological Reflection on the Christian Bible.* Minneapolis: Fortress, 1992.

———. *Introduction to the Old Testament as Scripture.* Philadelphia: Fortress, 1979.

———. "Walter Brueggemann's *Theology of the Old Testament: Testimony, Dispute, Advocacy.*" *Scottish Journal of Theology* 53 (2000) 228–33.

Clines, David J. A. *The Dictionary of Classical Hebrew.* Sheffield: Sheffield Academic, 1993.

———. *The Theme of the Pentateuch.* Journal for the Study of the Old Testament Supplement Series 10. Sheffield: JSOT Department of Biblical Studies, 1978.

Collins, John J. *Introduction to the Hebrew Bible.* Minneapolis: Fortress, 2004.

———. *A Short Introduction to the Hebrew Bible.* Minneapolis: Fortress, 2007.

Dever, *What Did the Biblical Writers Know and When Did They Know It? What Archaeology Can Tell Us About the Reality of Ancient Israel.* Grand Rapids: Eerdmans, 2001.

Dorrien, Gary. "Consolidating the Empire: Neoconservatism and the Politics of American Dominion." *Political Theology* 6 (2005) 409–28.

Dube, Musa W. *Postcolonial Feminist Interpretation of the Bible.* St. Louis: Chalice Press, 2000.

Ellul, Jacques. *The Humiliation of the Word.* Translated by Joyce Main Hanks. Grand Rapids: Eerdmans, 1985.

Fish, Stanley. "Rhetoric." In *Critical Terms for Literary Study,* edited by Frank Lentricchia and Thomas McLaughlin, 203–22. Chicago: University of Chicago Press, 1990.

Fleer, David, and Dave Bland, editors. *Preaching the Sermon on the Mount: The World It Imagines.* St. Louis: Chalice, 2007.

Freedman, David Noel, editor. *The Anchor Bible Dictionary.* 6 vols. New York: Doubleday, 1992.

———, editor. *Eerdmans Bible Dictionary.* Grand Rapids: Eerdmans, 2000.

Frick, Frank S. *The Formation of the State in Ancient Israel: A Survey of Models and Theories.* Social World in Biblical Antiquity 4. Sheffield: JSOT Press, 1985.

Gelzer, David George. "Mission to America being A History of the Work of the Basel Foreign Mission Society in America." Ph.d. dissertation, Yale University, 1952.

Gottwald, Norman K. "Social Matrix and Canonical Shape." *Theology Today* 42 (1985) 307–21.

———. *The Tribes of Yahweh: Sociology of the Religion of Liberated Israel, 1250–1050 B.C.E..* Maryknoll: Orbis, 1979.

Greene-McCreight, K. E. *Ad Litteram: How Augustine, Calvin, and Barth Read the "Plain Sense" of Genesis 1–3.* Issues in Systematic Theology 5. New York: Lang, 1999.

Hallo, William W., and William Kelly Simpson. *The Ancient Near East: A History.* 2nd ed. Fort Worth: Harcourt Brace College, 1998.

Hamilton, Jeffries M. *Social Justice and Deuteronomy: The Case of Deuteronomy 15.* Society of Biblical Literature Dissertation Series 136. Atlanta: Scholars, 1992.

Hanson, Paul D. *The Dawn of Apocalyptic: The Historical and Sociological Roots of Jewish Apocalyptic Eschatology.* Rev. ed. Philadelphia: Fortress, 1975.

Herman, Judith Lewis. *Trauma and Recovery: The Aftermath of Violence—from Domestic Abuse to Political Terror*. New York: Basic Books, 1992.

Hill, John. *Friend or Foe? The Figure of Babylon in the Book of Jeremiah MT*. Biblical Interpretation 40. Leiden: Brill, 1999.

Hooke, S. H. *Myth and Ritual: Essays on the Myth and Ritual of the Hebrews in Relation to the Culture Pattern of the Ancient Near East*. London: Oxford University Press, 1933.

————. *Myth, Ritual, and Kingship: Essays on the Theory and Practice of Kingship in the Ancient Near East and in Israel*. Oxford: Clarendon, 1958.

Joffe, Jacob. *Ueberpower: The Imperial Temptation of America*. New York: Norton, 2006.

Johnson, Chalmers. *Blowback: The Costs and Consequences of American Empire*. New York: Holt, 2000.

Kepnes, Steven. *The Text as Thou: Martin Buber's Dialogical Hermeneutics and Narrative Theology*. Bloomington: Indiana University Press, 1992.

Kermode, Frank. *The Sense of an Ending: Studies of the Theory of Fiction*. New York: Oxford University Press, 1967.

Koch, Klaus. "Is There a Doctrine of Retribution in the Old Testament?" In *Theodicy in the Old Testament*, edited by James L. Crenshaw, 57–87. Issues in Religion and Theology 4. Philadelphia: Fortress, 1983.

Kugel, James L. *How to Read the Bible: A Guide to Scripture, Then and Now*. New York: Free Press, 2007.

Lanham, Richard A. *The Motives of Eloquence: Literary Rhetoric in the Renaissance*. New Haven: Yale University Press, 1976.

Lapsley, Jacqueline E. "Feeling Our Way: Love for God in Deuteronomy." *Catholic Biblical Quarterly* 65 (2003) 350–69.

Levenson, Jon D. *The Hebrew Bible, the Old Testament, and Historical Criticism: Jews and Christians in Biblical Studies*. Louisville: Westminster John Knox, 1993.

————. *Sinai and Zion: An Entry into the Jewish Bible*. New York: Winston, 1985.

Lifton, Robert Jay. *Home from the War: Learning from Vietnam Veterans, with a New Preface and Epilogue on the Gulf War*. Boston: Beacon, 1991.

————. *The Nazi Doctors: Medical Killing and the Psychology of Genocide*. New York Basic Books, 1986.

Linafelt, Tod. *Ruth*. Berit Olam. Collegeville, MN: Liturgical, 1999.

————. *Surviving Lamentations: Catastrophe, Lament, and Protest in the Afterlife of a Biblical Book*. Chicago: University of Chicago Press, 2000.

Lincoln, Abraham. "Second Inaugural Address." In *Abraham Lincoln Speeches and Writings 1859–1865: Speeches, Letters, and Miscellaneous Writings Presidential Messages and Proclamations*, edited by Don E. Fehrenbacher, 687. New York: Library of America, 1989.

————. "To Thurlow Weed." In *Abraham Lincoln Speeches and Writings 1859–1865: Speeches, Letters, and Miscellaneous Writings Presidential Messages and Proclamations*, edited by Don E. Fehrenbacher, 689. New York: Library of America, 1989.

Lindbeck, George. *The Nature of Doctrine: Religion and Theology in a Postliberal Age*. Philadelphia: Westminster, 1984.

Lindström, Fredrik. *Suffering and Sin: Interpretations of Illness in the Individual Complaint Psalms.* Coniectanea Biblica: Old Testament Series 37. Stockholm: Almqvist & Wiksell, 1994.

Miles, Jack. *God: A Biography.* New York: Knopf, 1995.

Miller, J. Maxwell, and John H. Hayes. *A History of Ancient Israel and Judah.* Philadelphia: Westminster John Knox, 2006.

Miller, Patrick D. *Sin and Judgment in the Prophets: A Stylistic and Theological Analysis.* Society of Biblical Literature Monograph Series 27. Chico, CA: Scholars, 1982.

———. "'Slow to Anger': The God of the Prophets." In *The Way of the Lord: Essays in Old Testament Theology,* 269–85. Grand Rapids: Eerdmans, 2004.

———. *They Cried to the Lord: The Form and Theology of Biblical Prayer.* Minneapolis: Fortress, 1994.

Miranda, José P. *Marx and the Bible: A Critique of the Philosophy of Oppression.* 1974. Reprinted, Eugene, OR: Wipf & Stock, 2004.

Moltmann, Jürgen. *The Crucified God: The Cross of Christ as the Foundation and Criticism of Christian Theology.* Translated by R. A. Wilson and John Bowden. 1974. Reprinted, Minneapolis: Fortress, 1993.

Moran, William. "The Ancient Near Eastern Background of the Love of God in Deuteronomy." *Catholic Biblical Quarterly* 25 (1963) 77–87.

Muilenburg, James. "The Book of Isaiah, Chapters 40–66." In *The Interpreter's Bible,* edited by George A. Buttrick, 5:381–773. Nashville: Abingdon, 1956.

———. "Form Criticism and Beyond." *Journal of Biblical Literature* 88 (1968) 1–18.

Napier, B. Davie. *From Faith to Faith: Essays on Old Testament Literature.* New York: Harper & Brothers, 1955.

Noth, Martin. *A History of Pentateuchal Traditions.* Translated by Bernhard W. Anderson Englewood Cliffs, NJ: Prentice Hall, 1972.

O'Connor, Kathleen M. *Lamentations and the Tears of the World.* Maryknoll: Orbis, 2002.

Oppenheim, Michael. *Speaking/Writing of God: Jewish Philosophical Reflections on the Life with Others.* SUNY Series in Jewish Philosophy. Albany: SUNY Press, 1997.

Phillips, Kevin. *American Theocracy: The Perils and Politics of Radical Religion, Oil, and Borrowed Money in the 21st Century.* New York: Viking, 2006.

Polk, Timothy Houston. *The Biblical Kierkegaard: Reading by the Rule of Faith.* Macon: Mercer University Press, 1997.

Provan, Iain, V. Philips Long, and Tremper Longman III. *A Biblical History of Israel.* Louisville: Westminster John Knox, 2003.

Rad, Gerhard von. "The Joseph Narrative and Ancient Wisdom." In *From Genesis to Chronicles: Explorations in Old Testament Theology,* edited by K. C. Hanson, 75–81. Translated by E. W. Trueman Dicken. Fortress Classics in Biblical Studies. Minneapolis: Fortress, 2005.

———. *Old Testament Theology.* Vol. 1: *The Theology of Israel's Historical Traditions.* Translated by D. M. G. Stalker. New York: Harper & Row, 1962.

———. *Wisdom in Israel.* Translated by James D. Martin. Nashville: Abingdon, 1972.

Rendtorff, Rolf. *Canon and Theology: Overtures to an Old Testament Theology*. Translated and edited by Margaret Kohl. Overtures to Biblical Theology. Minneapolis: Fortress, 1993.

Ricoeur, Paul. "Biblical Hermeneutics." *Semeia* 4 (1975) 29–148.

———. *The Conflict of Interpretations: Essays in Hermeneutics*. Edited by Don Ihde. Evanston: Northwestern University Press, 1974.

———. *Essays on Biblical Interpretation*. Edited by Lewis S. Mudge. Philadelphia: Fortress, 1980.

———. *Freud and Philosophy: An Essay on Interpretation*. Translated by Denis Savage. New Haven: Yale University Press, 1970.

———. *Interpretation Theory: Discourse and the Surplus of Meaning*. Fort Worth: Texas Christian University Press, 1976.

———. *The Symbolism of Evil*. Translated by Emerson Buchanan. Boston: Beacon, 1967.

———. "Toward a Hermeneutic of the Idea of Revelation." In *Essays on Biblical Interpretation*, 73–118. Philadelphia: Fortress, 1980.

Rieger, Joerg. *Christ and Empire: From Paul to Postcolonial Times*. Minneapolis: Fortress, 2007.

Roberts, J. J. M. *Nahum, Habakkuk, and Zephaniah*. Old Testament Library. Louisville: Westminster John Knox, 1991.

Rorty, Richard. *Consequences of Pragmatism: Essays 1972–1980*. Minneapolis: University of Minnesota Press, 1982.

Rowland, Christopher, and Mark Corner, *Liberation Exegesis: The Challenge of Liberation Theology to Biblical Studies*. Louisville: Westminster John Knox, 1989.

Scarry, Elaine. *The Body in Pain: The Making and Unmaking of the World*. New York: Oxford University Press, 1985.

Schüssler Fiorenza, Elisabeth. *The Power of the Word: Scripture and the Rhetoric of Empire*. Minneapolis: Fortress, 2007.

Schwartz, Regina M. *The Curse of Cain: The Violent Legacy of Monotheism*. Chicago: Chicago University Press, 1997.

Searle, John R. *The Construction of Social Reality*. New York: The Free Press, 1995.

Smith, Daniel L. *The Religion of the Landless: The Social Context of the Babylonian Exile*. Bloomington: Meyer-Stone, 1989.

Smith, Mark S. *The Memoirs of God: History, Memory, and the Experience of the Divine in Ancient Israel*. Minneapolis: Fortress, 2004.

Smith, Morton. *Palestinian Parties and Politics that Shaped the Old Testament*. 2nd ed. London: SCM, 1987.

Smith-Christopher, Daniel L. *Biblical Theology of Exile*. Overtures to Biblical Theology. Minneapolis: Fortress, 2002.

Steussy, Marti J., editor. *Chalice Introduction to the Old Testament*. St. Louis: Chalice, 2003.

Stiver, Dan R. *Theology after Ricoeur: New Directions in Hermeneutical Theology*. Louisville: Westminster John Knox, 2001.

Stuhlmacher, Peter. *How to Do Biblical Theology*. Princeton Theological Monograph Series 38. Allison Park, PA: Pickwick, 1995.

Sugurtharajah, R. S. *Postcolonial Criticism and Biblical Interpretation*. Oxford: Oxford University Press, 2002.

Talen, Bill. *What Should I Do If Reverend Billy Is in My Store?* New York: The New Press, 2003.

Terrien, Samuel. *The Elusive Presence: Toward a New Biblical Theology*. 1978. Reprinted, Eugene, OR: Wipf & Stock, 2000.

Thiel, John E. *Nonfoundationalism*. Guides to Theological Inquiry. Minneapolis: Fortress, 1994.

Tracy, David. *The Analogical Imagination: Christian Theology and the Culture of Pluralism*. New York: Crossroad, 1981.

Trible, Phyllis. *God and the Rhetoric of Sexuality*. Overtures to Biblical Theology. Philadelphia: Fortress, 1978.

———. *Rhetorical Criticism: Context, Method, and the Book of Jonah*. Guides to Biblical Scholarship. Minneapolis: Fortress, 1994.

Wallace, Mark I. *The Second Naiveté: Barth, Ricoeur, and the New Yale School*. 2nd ed. Studies in American Biblical Hermeneutics 6. Macon: Mercer University Press, 1995.

Whitaker, Richard E. *The Eerdmans Analytical Concordance to the Revised Standard Version of the Bible*. Grand Rapids: Eerdmans, 1988.

White, James Boyd. *Living Speech: Resisting the Empire of Force*. Princeton: Princeton University Press, 2006.

Wilken, Robert L., editor. *Isaiah: Interpreted by Early Church and Medieval Commentators*. The Church's Bible. Grand Rapids: Eerdmans, 2007.

Wilson, Robert R. *Prophecy and Society in Ancient Israel*. Philadelphia: Fortress, 1980.

Yerushalmi, Yosef Hayim. *Zakhor: Jewish History and Jewish Memory*. Seattle: Washington University Press, 1982.

Young, Jeremy. *The Violence of God and the War on Terror*. London: Darton, Longman and Todd, 2007.

Young, Robert. *Analytical Concordance to the Holy Bible*. Nashville: Abingdon, 1982.

SCRIPTURE INDEX

Old Testament

~